ARM 55 Course Guide

Risk Assessment and Treatment
1st Edition

The Institutes
720 Providence Road, Suite 100
Malvern, Pennsylvania 19355-3433

1st Edition • 2nd Printing • March 2015

ISBN 978-0-89463-618-9

Contents

 ## Study Materials Available for ARM 55

Risk Assessment and Treatment, 1st ed., 2012, AICPCU.

ARM 55 *Course Guide*, 1st ed., 2012, AICPCU (includes access code for SMART Online Practice Exams).

ARM 55 SMART Study Aids—Review Notes and Flash Cards, 1st ed.

Student Resources

Catalog A complete listing of our offerings can be found in The Institutes' professional development catalog, including information about:

- Current programs and courses
- Current textbooks, course guides, SMART Study Aids, and online offerings
- Program completion requirements
- Exam registration

To obtain a copy of the catalog, visit our website at www.TheInstitutes.org or contact Customer Service at (800) 644-2101.

How to Prepare for Institutes Exams This free handbook is designed to help you by:

- Giving you ideas on how to use textbooks and course guides as effective learning tools
- Providing steps for answering exam questions effectively
- Recommending exam-day strategies

The handbook is printable from the Student Services Center on The Institutes' website at www.TheInstitutes.org or available by calling Customer Service at (800) 644-2101.

Educational Counseling Services To ensure that you take courses matching both your needs and your skills, you can obtain free counseling from The Institutes by:

- Emailing your questions to advising@TheInstitutes.org
- Calling an Institutes' counselor directly at (610) 644-2100, ext. 7601
- Obtaining and completing a self-inventory form, available on our website at www.TheInstitutes.org or by contacting Customer Service at (800) 644-2101

Exam Registration Information As you proceed with your studies, be sure to arrange for your exam.

- Visit our website at www.TheInstitutes.org/forms to access and print the Registration Booklet, which contains information and forms needed to register for your exam.
- Plan to register with The Institutes well in advance of your exam.

How to Contact The Institutes For more information on any of these publications and services:

- Visit our website at www.TheInstitutes.org
- Call us at (800) 644-2101 or (610) 644-2100 outside the U.S.
- Email us at customerservice@TheInstitutes.org
- Fax us at (610) 640-9576
- Write to us at The Institutes, Customer Service, 720 Providence Road, Suite 100, Malvern, PA 19355-3433

Using This Course Guide

This course guide will help you learn the course content and prepare for the exam.

Each assignment in this course guide typically includes the following components:

Educational Objectives These are the most important study tools in the course guide. Because all of the questions on the exam are based on the Educational Objectives, the best way to study for the exam is to focus on these objectives.

Each Educational Objective typically begins with one of the following action words, which indicate the level of understanding required for the exam:

Analyze—Determine the nature and the relationship of the parts.

Apply—Put to use for a practical purpose.

Associate—Bring together into relationship.

Calculate—Determine numeric values by mathematical process.

Classify—Arrange or organize according to class or category.

Compare—Show similarities and differences.

Contrast—Show only differences.

Define—Give a clear, concise meaning.

Describe—Represent or give an account.

Determine—Settle or decide.

Evaluate—Determine the value or merit.

Explain—Relate the importance or application.

Identify or list—Name or make a list.

Illustrate—Give an example.

Justify—Show to be right or reasonable.

Paraphrase—Restate in your own words.

Recommend—Suggest or endorse something to be used.

Summarize—Concisely state the main points.

Outline The outline lists the topics in the assignment. Read the outline before the required reading to become familiar with the assignment content and the relationships of topics.

Key Words and Phrases These words and phrases are fundamental to understanding the assignment and have a common meaning for those working in insurance. After completing the required reading, test your understanding of the assignment's Key Words and Phrases by writing their definitions.

Review Questions The review questions test your understanding of what you have read. Review the Educational Objectives and required reading, then answer the questions to the best of your ability. When you are finished, check the answers at the end of the assignment to evaluate your comprehension.

Application Questions These questions continue to test your knowledge of the required reading by applying what you've studied to "hypothetical" real-life situations. Again, check the suggested answers at the end of the assignment to review your progress.

Sample Exam Your course guide includes a sample exam (located at the back) or a code for accessing SMART Online Practice Exams (which appears on the inside of the cover). Use the option available for the course you're taking to become familiar with the test format.

For courses that offer SMART Online Practice Exams, you can either download and print a sample credentialing exam or take full practice exams using questions like those that will appear on your credentialing exam. SMART Online Practice Exams are as close as you can get to experiencing an actual exam before taking one.

More Study Aids

The Institutes also produce supplemental study tools, called SMART Study Aids, for many of our courses. When SMART Study Aids are available for a course, they are listed on page iii of the course guide. SMART Study Aids include Review Notes and Flash Cards and are excellent tools to help you learn and retain the information in each assignment.

A

Direct Your Learning

Introduction to Risk Assessment and Treatment

Educational Objectives

After learning the content of this assignment, you should be able to:

1. Describe the nature of risk assessment and the risk assessment process.

2. Describe the major risk identification and analysis techniques.

3. Describe the risk treatment process and risk treatment techniques.

4. Describe the following accident analysis techniques:

   - Sequence of events (domino theory)

   - Energy transfer theory

   - Technique of operations review (TOR) approach

   - Change analysis

   - Job-safety analysis

5. Describe system safety, its primary purpose, and its advantages.

6. Explain how to implement the following loss control techniques for hazard risk:

   - Avoidance

   - Loss prevention

   - Loss reduction

   - Separation, duplication, and diversification

Outline

▶ **Overview of Risk Assessment**
  A. Risk Assessment Defined
  B. Goals of Risk Assessment
  C. Risk Assessment Process
    1. Risk Identification
    2. Risk Analysis

▶ **Categories of Risk Identification and Analysis Techniques**
  A. Questionnaires and Checklists
  B. Workshops
  C. Cause and Effect Analysis
  D. Failure Analysis
    1. Hazard and Operability Studies (HAZOP)
    2. Fault Tree Analysis (FTA)
    3. Failure Mode and Effects Analysis (FMEA)
  E. Future States Analysis
  F. Strategy Analysis

▶ **Risk Treatment**
  A. Risk Treatment Process
  B. Risk Treatment Techniques

▶ **Traditional Accident Analysis Techniques**
  A. Accident Causation
  B. Accident Analysis Techniques
    1. Sequence of Events (Domino Theory)
    2. Energy Transfer Theory
    3. Technique of Operations Review (TOR) Approach
    4. Change Analysis
    5. Job Safety Analysis

▶ **System Safety Analysis**
  A. System Safety Defined
  B. The Concept of a System
    1. Components
    2. Purpose
    3. Environment
    4. Life Cycle
  C. System Safety Example
  D. System Safety Advantages

▶ **Loss Control Techniques for Hazard Risk**
  A. Avoidance
  B. Loss Prevention
  C. Loss Reduction
  D. Separation, Duplication, and Diversification

s.m.a.r.t. tips

Don't spend time on material you have already mastered. The SMART Review Notes are organized by the Educational Objectives found in each assignment to help you track your study.

For each assignment, you should define or describe each of the Key Words and Phrases and answer each of the Review and Application Questions.

Educational Objective 1
Describe the nature of risk assessment and the risk assessment process.

Key Words and Phrases

Risk

Risk management

Risk map

Review Questions

1-1. Identify the two steps in the risk assessment process.

1-2. Describe the goals of risk assessment.

1-3. Contrast qualitative risk assessment techniques with quantitative risk assessment techniques.

1-4. Describe the risk identification process.

Educational Objective 2
Describe the major risk identification and analysis techniques.

Review Questions

2-1. Describe two disadvantages of using questionnaires and checklists as a risk identification technique.

2-2. Describe the Delphi risk identification technique.

2-3. Identify two approaches to cause and effect analysis.

2-4. List a disadvantage of the cause and effect analysis technique.

2-5. Describe the hazard and operability studies (HAZOP) technique.

2-6. Describe the scenario analysis risk assessment technique.

Educational Objective 3
Describe the risk treatment process and risk treatment techniques.

Key Words and Phrases
Residual risk

Speculative risk

Pure risk

Avoidance

Loss prevention

Loss reduction

Retention

Review Questions

3-1. Describe the goal of risk treatment.

3-2. Explain why it is important to monitor risk treatment plans.

3-3. List the general categories of risk treatment options.

3-4. Describe risk treatment techniques for events that appear to have primarily positive potential outcomes.

Educational Objective 4

Describe the following accident analysis techniques:

- **Sequence of events (domino theory)**
- **Energy transfer theory**
- **Technique of operations review (TOR) approach**
- **Change analysis**
- **Job-safety analysis**

Key Words and Phrases

Domino theory

Energy transfer theory

Technique of operations review (TOR)

Change analysis

Job safety analysis (JSA)

Review Questions

4-1. Describe the basic causes of most accidents.

4-2. Identify the chain of accident factors contained in the domino theory.

▶▶

4-3. Identify the situations to which the domino theory is most applicable.

4-4. List the five basic principles of risk control under the technique of operations review (TOR) approach.

4-5. Describe the change analysis approach to accident causation.

Application Question

4-6. Sam, a twenty-five-year-old house painter employed by Acme Construction Company, was injured while painting the gutters of a nearly completed new house. Working fast to finish before quitting time, Sam reached to his far left to finish the last section rather than taking the time to climb down and move the ladder. Because Sam inadequately braced the ladder, and because the apprentice who worked with Sam was out sick and everyone else was too busy to watch the ladder, no one noticed when the base of the ladder slipped out to Sam's right. As the ladder fell, Sam caught himself on the gutter with his right hand but—after hanging there for a few seconds—dropped to the ground as the gutter gave way under his weight. Although the collapsing gutter slowed his fall, Sam landed crookedly—his right hand extended above his head, his left leg hitting the ground first. Describe how each of the following theories would apply to this loss:

a.   Domino theory

b.   Energy transfer theory

c.   The technique of operations review (TOR) approach

Educational Objective 5
Describe system safety, its primary purpose, and its advantages.

Key Words and Phrases
System safety

Conceptual phase

▶▶

Engineering phase

Production phase

Operational phase

Disposal phase

Review Questions

5-1. Explain how system safety analysis is used to identify potential sources of loss.

5-2. List the four features of a system.

5-3. Identify the components of a system.

5-4. Explain how a risk management professional protects the integrity of an organization's systems.

5-5. Describe the five phases in the life cycle of any system.

5-6. Describe the three advantages of applying systems safety to loss control programs.

▶▶

Application Question

5-7. A passenger seated on a moving United States passenger train suffered a broken leg when the train came to a sudden halt, throwing the passenger against the back of the seat in front of him. Assume that the train stopped because the engineer pulled the emergency stop cord as soon as he saw an automobile sitting on the tracks at a crossing approximately 100 yards ahead. Describe the nature and/or causes of this passenger's broken leg in terms of three levels of subsystems within successively larger systems.

Educational Objective 6

Explain how to implement the following loss control techniques for hazard risk:

- **Avoidance**
- **Loss prevention**
- **Loss reduction**
- **Separation, duplication, and diversification**

Key Words and Phrases

Avoidance

Separation

Duplication

Diversification

Review Questions

6-1. Contrast loss prevention with loss reduction.

6-2. Explain why loss prevention measures are generally implemented before an accident occurs.

6-3. Describe the two categories of loss reduction measures.

6-4. Describe the circumstances required for separation to be an appropriate loss control technique.

Answers to Assignment 1 Questions

NOTE: These answers are provided to give students a basic understanding of acceptable types of responses. They often are not the only valid answers and are not intended to provide an exhaustive response to the questions.

Educational Objective 1

1-1.   The risk assessment process consists of these steps:

- Risk identification

- Risk analysis

1-2.   The goals of risk assessment are to inform management at all levels of the risks facing an organization and how those risks affect the organization's ability to meet objectives, as well as to identify potential risk treatment options.

1-3.   Qualitative risk assessment techniques, such as surveys or interviews, are more subjective and open to interpretation. Quantitative assessments are objective and based on numerical data and calculations.

1-4.   Risk identification involves reviewing all aspects of the internal and external environments to identify events that could either improve or inhibit the organization's achievement of objectives. It is important at this step to uncover a complete inventory of possible risks to avoid the consequences arising from an unidentified risk in the future.

Educational Objective 2

2-1.   One disadvantage of questionnaires and checklists is that they do not produce quantitative results. A second disadvantage is that, because of the format of these techniques, not all risks may be identified, and potential problems may be overlooked.

2-2.   The Delphi technique is a form of brainstorming that relies on a panel of experts to reach a consensus opinion on an issue. A team is formed to select the panel of experts and to monitor the process. The team sends the experts a semi-structured questionnaire, which the experts respond to anonymously.

2-3.   Two approaches to cause and effect analysis include the fishbone diagram and the 5 Whys technique.

2-4.   A disadvantage of the cause and effect analysis technique is that participants may stop the process before all underlying causes have been identified and examined, which can result in a failure to accurately uncover the true root cause of the issue under analysis.

2-5.   The HAZOP technique uses a team of specialists from different operational areas to study a process or procedure to examine how failures can result in a hazard.

2-6.   Scenario analysis is a future states analysis approach that is used to examine how the current environment may be influenced by emerging developments, such as new technology or new competitors entering the market. With this approach, a team is formed to consider changes or major trends and to develop various scenarios to develop possible outcomes. Based on these outcomes, risks can be identified, analyzed, and evaluated.

▶▶

Educational Objective 3

3-1. The goal of risk treatment is to modify identified risks to assist the organization in meeting its objectives.

3-2. Review of risk treatment plans is important because risks may change based on the organization's operation or on environmental factors, such as economic conditions or legal and regulatory requirements. Previous risk treatment decisions may no longer be valid, and implemented controls may no longer be effective. Furthermore, emerging risks such as those arising from new technology or the acquisition of a new business unit must be identified and assessed, and a cost-benefit analysis should be conducted to assess whether the benefits of the chosen treatment option continue to outweigh related costs.

3-3. In general, available risk treatment options fall into the categories of avoidance, modification, transfer, retention, or exploitation.

3-4. For events that appear to have primarily positive potential outcomes, risk treatment techniques would focus on exploiting the risk by maximizing expected gains. Techniques would include modifying the likelihood of an event to increase the opportunity to meet objectives while also considering treatment options for potential negative outcomes.

Educational Objective 4

4-1. The basic causes of most accidents are poor management, safety policy, and personal or environmental factors.

4-2. This is the chain of accident factors in the domino theory:

- Ancestry and social environment

- Fault of person

- An unsafe act and/or a mechanical or physical hazard

- The accident itself

- The resulting injury

4-3. Because of its emphasis on human fault, the domino theory is most applicable to situations within human control.

4-4. These are the five basic principles of risk control under the TOR approach:

- An unsafe act, an unsafe condition, and an accident are all symptoms of something wrong in the management system.

- Certain circumstances, unless identified and controlled, will produce severe injuries.

- Safety should be managed like any other organizational function, with management setting achievable goals and planning, organizing, leading, and controlling to achieve them.

- Management must specify procedures for accountability if safety efforts are to be effective.

- The function of safety is to locate and define the operational errors that allow accidents to occur.

4-5. The change analysis approach to analyzing the cause of accidents asks a series of "what if" questions and projects the consequences for each of the changes and for all feasible combinations of change.

4-6. These answers apply to the Acme Construction case:

a. H.W. Heinrich, who developed the domino theory, described each of the five accident factors as a domino, emphasizing that every accident sequence begins with a negative ancestry or social environment for a person and ends with an injury or illness. Sam's unsafe action, reaching too far, precipitated a series of events that resulted in his injury. A number of other actions contributed to, and resulted in, Sam's awkward fall.

b. The energy transfer theory approach for preventing accidents or reducing the resulting harm focuses on controlling released energy and/or reducing the harm caused by that energy. As the ladder fell, the energy released Sam's weight and the upright ladder, resulting in disequilibrium.

c. In the TOR approach, managers must recognize their own (or their colleagues' or subordinates') faults and correct them. Removing these management faults will eliminate most, if not all, accidents. For Sam's injury, the management failure was not designating who had the clear responsibility to substitute for the apprentice who was out sick.

Educational Objective 5

5-1. System safety analysis looks at an organization as a whole to identify potential sources of losses. An accident occurs when a component of a system malfunctions. System safety predicts how these malfunctions might occur so that appropriate action can be taken either to prevent the failure or to reduce its consequences.

5-2. All systems have these four features:

*   Components
*   Purpose
*   Environment
*   Life cycle

5-3. These are the components of a system:

*   Physical elements
*   Subsystems
*   Energy sources

5-4. To protect the integrity of an organization's systems, a risk management professional must protect the ability of a system's parts to move as planned, ensure a reliable source of energy to power the organization's systems when needed, and guard against this energy's escaping and causing harm.

▶▶

5-5. These are the five phases that occur in the life cycle of any system:

- Conceptual phase, when the basic purpose and preliminary design of the system are formulated.

- Engineering phase, when the actual system is created.

- Production phase, involves creating the system according to the dimensions, specifications, and procedures determined in a prior phase.

- Operational phase, when the system is implemented.

- Disposal phase, when the system reaches the end of its useful life.

5-6. These are the advantages of applying system safety to loss control programs:

- By considering how an accident impairs various systems, risk management professionals can follow an orderly process for developing a range of loss control measures that improve the reliability of interrelated systems.

- Because systems differ in scope, risk management professionals can use system safety analysis to enlist the cooperation of many people inside and outside the organization.

- By using a system safety approach, risk management professionals can reduce accident frequency and severity by defining and preventing events that lead to a particular type of accident.

5-7. The passenger broke his leg because he was propelled forward with great force against a train seat. The passenger was contained within the subsystem of the train car. The train car itself is a subsystem of the train, which, with its locomotive engine, is pulling all the cars down the tracks. The train is a subsystem of the larger system of the railroad. In a more general way, this subsystem is contained within the entire transportation system of the U.S. As an independently operated vehicle, the automobile the train was braking for was also part of the transportation system.

Educational Objective 6

6-1. Loss prevention is a loss control technique that reduces the frequency of a particular loss without necessarily affecting loss severity. Loss reduction is a loss control technique that reduces the severity of a particular loss.

6-2. Loss prevention measures are generally implemented before an accident occurs to break the sequence of events that lead to the accident. Breaking the sequence should prevent the accident from occurring or at least make it less likely.

6-3. The two broad categories of loss reduction measures are pre-loss measures (applied before the loss occurs) and post-loss measures (applied after the loss occurs).

6-4. Separation is a loss control technique that disperses a particular asset or activity over several locations and regularly relies on that asset or activity as part of the organization's resources. Separation is appropriate if an organization can operate with only a portion of these separate units intact. If one unit suffers a total loss, the portion of the assets or operations in the other unit must be sufficient for operations to continue. Each of the separated units is normally kept in daily use.

Direct Your Learning

Root Cause Analysis

Educational Objectives

After learning the content of this assignment, you should be able to:

1. Describe root cause analysis and the steps in the root cause analysis process.

2. Explain how an organization can use failure mode and effects analysis (FMEA) to assess and mitigate risk.

3. Explain how an organization can use fault tree analysis (FTA) to determine the causes of a risk event.

4. Explain how an organization can use a "5 Whys" analysis and fishbone (Ishikawa) diagram to determine the causes of a risk event.

Outline

▶ **Introduction to Root Cause Analysis**
  A. The Nature of Root Cause Analysis
  B. Steps in the Root Cause Analysis Process
  C. Root Cause Analysis Example
▶ **Failure Mode and Effects Analysis (FMEA)**
  A. Steps in the FMEA Process
  B. FMEA Example
  C. Advantages and Disadvantages
▶ **Fault Tree Analysis (FTA)**
  A. The Nature of Fault Tree Analysis (FTA)
  B. Adding Probabilities to a Fault Tree
  C. Application to Loss Control
  D. Assumptions and Limitations
▶ **"5 Whys" Analysis and the Fishbone Diagram**
  A. 5 Whys Analysis
    1. Procedure for Conducting a 5 Whys Analysis
    2. 5 Whys Example
    3. Advantages and Disadvantages of 5 Whys Analysis
  B. The Fishbone Diagram
    1. Steps in Developing a Fishbone Diagram
    2. Fishbone Diagram Example

s.m.a.r.t. tips   Reduce the number of Key Words and Phrases that you must review. SMART Flash Cards contain the Key Words and Phrases and their definitions, allowing you to set aside those cards that you have mastered.

▶▶

For each assignment, you should define or describe each of the Key Words and Phrases and answer each of the Review and Application Questions.

Educational Objective 1

Describe root cause analysis and the steps in the root cause analysis process.

Key Words and Phrases

Root cause

Root cause analysis (RCA)

Causal factors

Review Questions

1-1. Identify the purpose of root cause analysis.

1-2. Identify the four basic characteristics of root causes.

1-3. Identify the sources of organizational causes of loss.

1-4. Identify the five broadly defined root cause analysis approaches.

1-5. Identify the purpose of casual factors charting.

Educational Objective 2

Explain how an organization can use failure mode and effects analysis (FMEA) to assess and mitigate risk.

Key Words and Phrases

Failure mode and effects analysis (FMEA)

Failure mode

Effects analysis

Indenture level

Local effect

Next-higher-level effect

End effect

Criticality analysis

Risk priority number (RPN)

Criticality

Fault tree analysis (FTA)

Review Questions

2-1. Identify the outputs of failure mode and effects analysis (FMEA).

2-2. Identify the steps in the FMEA process.

2-3. Identify examples of types of FMEA.

2-4. Identify the components of a risk priority number.

2-5. Identify the advantages of using FMEA.

▶▶

2-6. Identify the disadvantages of using FMEA.

Educational Objective 3
Explain how an organization can use fault tree analysis (FTA) to determine the causes of a risk event.

Review Questions

3-1. Identify the goals of fault tree analysis.

3-2. Identify the function of a fault tree's gates.

3-3. Identify the function of a fault tree's rectangles.

3-4. Explain what an "or" gate signifies.

3-5. Identify the characteristics of a fault tree that encourage sound loss control decisions.

3-6. Identify the limitations of fault tree analysis.

Educational Objective 4

Explain how an organization can use a "5 Whys" analysis and fishbone (Ishikawa) diagram to determine the causes of a risk event.

Review Questions

4-1. Describe a "5 Whys" analysis.

4-2. Identify the steps in a 5 Whys analysis.

4-3. Identify the advantages of a 5 Whys analysis.

4-4. Identify the disadvantages of a 5 Whys analysis.

4-5. Identify the categories included in the 6 Ms group of categories.

4-6. Identify the steps in developing a fishbone diagram.

Answers to Assignment 2 Questions

NOTE: These answers are provided to give students a basic understanding of acceptable types of responses. They often are not the only valid answers and are not intended to provide an exhaustive response to the questions.

Educational Objective 1

1-1. The purpose of root cause analysis is to determine the underlying cause of a harmful event.

1-2. These are the four basic characteristics of root causes:

- A root cause is expressed as a specific underlying cause, not as a generalization.

- A root cause can be reasonably identified.

- A root cause must be expressed as something that can be modified.

- A root cause must produce effective recommendations for prevention of future accidents that stem from the root cause.

1-3. Organizational causes of loss stem from faulty systems, processes, or policies (such as procedures that do not make it clear which maintenance employee is responsible for checking and maintaining the manufacturer's production line).

1-4. These are the five broadly defined root cause analysis approaches:

- Safety-based

- Production-based

- Process-based

- Failure-based

- Systems-based

1-5. The purpose of causal factors charting is to provide the structure to organize and analyze the data gathered during the investigation. It also helps to identify gaps and deficiencies in knowledge as the investigation progresses.

Educational Objective 2

2-1. These are the outputs of failure mode and effects analysis (FMEA):

- Improvement in the design of procedures and processes

- Minimization or elimination of design characteristics that contribute to failure

- Development of system requirements that reduce the likelihood of failures

- Identification of human error modes and their effects

- Development of systems to track and manage potential future design problems

2-2. These are the steps in the FMEA process:

- Define FMEA study in scope and objective(s)

- Assemble team to perform FMEA

- Break down system into components

- Define function of each component

- For each component listed, identify the way each part could conceivably fail, the mechanism that might produce those failure modes, the effect if failure occurs, the extent of failure, and when/how failure is detected

- Develop provisions in design to compensate for failure

2-3. These are examples of types of FMEA:

- Concept

- Design

- Process

- Equipment

- Service

- System

- Software

2-4. These are the components of a risk priority number:

- Consequence rankings

- Occurrence rankings

- Detection rankings

2-5. These are the advantages of using FMEA:

- It is widely applicable to human, equipment, and system failure modes and to hardware and software procedures.

- When used early in the design phase, it can reduce costly equipment modifications.

- It can improve the quality, reliability, and safety of a product or process, as well as improve an organization's image and competitiveness by possibly reducing scrap in production.

- It emphasizes problem prevention by identifying problems early in the process and eliminating potential failure modes.

2-6. These are the disadvantages of using FMEA:

- When used as a top-down tool, FMEA may only identify major failure modes in a system.

- Other analysis methods might be better suited for this type of analysis. When used as a bottom-up tool, it can complement other methods, such as fault tree analysis, and identify more failure modes resulting in top-level symptoms.

- Analyzing complex multilayered systems can be difficult and tedious with FMEA, and studies that are not adequately controlled and focused can be time-consuming and costly.

Educational Objective 3

3-1. The goals of fault tree analysis are to examine the conditions that may have led to or influenced a risk event, identify potential accidents, and predict the most likely system failures.

3-2. The function of a fault tree's gates is to represent the causal relationships between events.

3-3. The function of a fault tree's rectangles is to depict events.

3-4. An "or" gate signifies that any one of the events leading to the gate is sufficient to cause that event.

3-5. To encourage sound loss control decisions, a fault tree must be as complete and accurate as possible. An incomplete fault tree may entirely omit a chain of events that would make loss control measures applied to some other tree branch ineffective.

3-6. These are the limitations of fault tree analysis:

- If a high degree of certainty does not exist concerning the probabilities of the underlying or base events, the probability of the top event may also be uncertain.

- Important pathways to the top event might not be explored if all causal events are not included in the fault tree.

- Because a fault tree is static, it may need to be reconstructed in the future if circumstances or procedures change.

- Human error is difficult to characterize in a fault tree.

- "Domino effects" or conditional failures are not easily included in a fault tree.

Educational Objective 4

4-1. A 5 Whys analysis is a specific root cause analysis technique used primarily for problems involving human factors, such as lack of managerial oversight.

4-2. These are the steps in a 5 Whys analysis:

- The specific problem under investigation is described completely.

- The investigator asks why that particular problem occurred and determines the answer.

- If the answer does not reveal the problem's root cause, the investigator determines why the problem embodied by the determination made in Step 2 occurred.

- The investigator repeats the previous two steps until the root cause of the original problem has been determined.

4-3. These are the advantages of a 5 Whys analysis:

- It can determine the root cause of a problem.

- When several root causes are found, it can help determine the relationship among them.

- It usually does not require statistical analysis or data collection.

4-4. These are the disadvantages of a 5 Whys analysis:

- Investigators tend to stop the analysis after the first determination rather than asking additional questions to discover a problem's root cause.

- Investigators tend to focus on only one answer to each question.

- Organizations sometimes do not help the investigator ask the right why questions.

- An uninformed investigator cannot ask relevant questions.

- Different investigators will discover different causes for the same problem.

4-5. These are the categories included in the 6 Ms group of categories:

- Machine (technology)

- Method (process)

- Materials

- Manpower (physical work)/mindpower (brain work)

- Measurement (inspection)

- Milieu/Mother Nature (environment)

4-6. These are the steps in developing a fishbone diagram:

- Team agrees on a problem statement.

- Facilitator writes statement on the far-right-hand side of the diagram, draws a box or circle around it, and draws a horizontal arrow across the center of the page that points to the statement.

- Team brainstorms the major categories of causes of the problem.

- Facilitator depicts the categories of causes as branches emanating from the main arrow.

- Team members brainstorm possible specific causes of the problem, using techniques such as the 5 Whys analysis.

- Facilitator writes each specific cause as a branch from the appropriate category. Causes can be assigned to any category to which they relate.

- For each of the specific causes listed in the previous step, the team again asks, "Why did this happen?" The facilitator writes the sub-causes as branches from the causes. The team continues to ask why to generate deeper levels of causes. As the layers of branches are drawn on the diagram, causal relationships are revealed.

- Before moving to the final step, the team should focus on areas of the diagram with the fewest ideas.

- Once the team has determined the root cause(s), remedies are developed and implemented to prevent recurrence of the problem described in the original statement.

Direct Your Learning

Business Continuity Management

Educational Objectives

After learning the content of this assignment, you should be able to:

1. Describe the evolution of business continuity management and its alignment with risk management.

2. Explain how risk mitigation is achieved through business continuity planning.

3. Describe the scope and stages of strategic risk redeployment planning.

4. Explain how supply chain risk management is used to assess and mitigate risks that could disrupt an organization's flow of goods and services.

5. Explain how risk mitigation is achieved through efficient communication in times of crisis.

6. Given a scenario involving a supply chain, recommend the risk-appropriate mitigation tools.

Outline

▶ **Introduction to Business Continuity Management**

  A. Evolution of BCM

  B. Aligning Business Continuity Management With Risk Management

  C. Business Continuity Certifications and Standards

▶ **Business Continuity Planning**

  A. Understanding the Business

  B. Conducting a Business Impact Analysis

  C. Performing a Risk Assessment

  D. Developing the Continuity Plan

  E. Implementing the Continuity Plan

  F. Building a BCM/BCP Culture

  G. Maintaining and Updating the Plan

▶ **Strategic Redeployment Planning**

  A. Strategic Redeployment Planning Stages

  B. Emergency Stage

  C. Alternate Marketing Stage

  D. Contingency Production Stage

  E. Communication Stage

  F. Conditions for Success

▶ **Supply Chain Risk Management**

  A. Threats and Opportunities Inherent in Supply Chains

  B. Balance Between Efficiency and Vulnerability to Disruptions

  C. Supply Chain Best Practices

▶ **Crisis Communication**

  A. Mitigating Risk Through Crisis Communication

  B. Stakeholder Communications

    1. Internal Stakeholders

    2. External Stakeholders

  C. Benefits of Crisis Communication

▶ **Mitigating Supply Chain Risk**

  A. Case Facts

  B. Case Analysis Tools

  C. Overview of Analysis

    1. Exposure Identification

  D. Determination of Co-Dependencies

    1. Analysis of Exposures

s.m.a.r.t. tips

Actively capture information by using the open space in the SMART Review Notes to write out key concepts. Putting information into your own words is an effective way to push that information into your memory.

▶▶

For each assignment, you should define or describe each of the Key Words and Phrases and answer each of the Review and Application Questions.

Educational Objective 1
Describe the evolution of business continuity management and its alignment with risk management.

Review Questions

1-1. Describe the objective of business continuity management (BCM).

1-2. Compare and contrast risk management and business continuity management.

1-3. Describe in general terms the objectives of the three internationally recognized standards that promote private-sector preparedness, adopted by the United States Department of Homeland Security.

Educational Objective 2

Explain how risk mitigation is achieved through business continuity planning.

Review Questions

2-1. Describe how developing a business continuity plan can help an organization.

2-2. Describe the role of a business impact analysis (BIA) in business continuity planning.

2-3. Describe the following strategies used in continuity planning:

   a.   Active back-up model

   b.   Split operations model

c.   Alternative site model

d.   Contingency model

2-4.   Describe the roles of senior management in establishing a business continuity management (BCM)/business continuity plan (BCP) culture.

Educational Objective 3
Describe the scope and stages of strategic risk redeployment planning.

Review Questions

3-1.   Identify the four stages of a strategic redeployment plan.

3-2. Describe the three objectives of the emergency stage of a strategic redeployment plan.

3-3. Summarize the alternate marketing stage of a strategic redeployment plan.

3-4. Describe the considerations an organization must address during the contingency production stage.

3-5. Identify the sole objective of the communication stage.

Educational Objective 4

Explain how supply chain risk management is used to assess and mitigate risks that could disrupt an organization's flow of goods and services.

Review Questions

4-1. Define supply chain risk management as it applies to the production of goods and provision of services.

4-2. Describe six internal supply chain exposures and vulnerabilities.

4-3. Describe eight external supply chain exposures and vulnerabilities.

4-4. Describe the process for establishing supply chain best practices.

Educational Objective 5
Explain how risk mitigation is achieved through efficient communication in times of crisis.

Review Questions

5-1. Identify the attributes of a good stakeholder crisis communications plan.

5-2. Identify communication that should be directed specifically to internal stakeholders during and following a crisis.

5-3. Identify communication that should be directed specifically to external stakeholders during and following a crisis.

Educational Objective 6

Given a scenario involving a supply chain, recommend the risk-appropriate mitigation tools.

Application Question

6-1. Southern Bend Ranch, located along Texas's Colorado River, is a producer of organic beef and venison. It uses a combination of grass/forage feeding and ranch-grown supplemental organic grain to produce a uniquely favorable and tender meat, and it is one of only a few producers of this type of meat in Texas.

Southern Bend Ranch sells approximately 85 percent of its beef and venison to one primary customer, Whole Organic Meat Market in Houston. Southern Bend is Whole Organic's sole supplier of beef and venison.

Southern Bend's contract with Whole Organic outlines the parameters in which the beef and venison will be produced as well as the amount of meat that will be supplied. If either of these sets of parameters is not met, the contract defines penalties that Southern Bend Ranch will have to pay. The contract is silent on "acts of God."

The Colorado River, on the southern border of Southern Bend Ranch, has a series of flood-control dams upstream. One spring, the quasi-government entity (QGE) in charge of monitoring the water flow failed to anticipate the effects of a heavy rainfall upstream, including the resulting flooding of the lakes above and between the dams. To prevent flooding the expensive homes surrounding one of the lakes, QGE released water from the lake. As a result, properties farther downstream were flooded. The flooding caused nonorganic pollutants to wash downriver onto part of the ranch.

Southern Bend Ranch informed Whole Organic that its shipments of meat would be cut in half because 50 percent of its herds, grass/forage, and feed had been contaminated by the nonorganic pollutants from the flood. Whole Organic demanded that Southern Bend pay the penalties stipulated in the contract. Southern Bend Ranch countered that because the flood was an act of God, the ranch is not responsible. Lawsuits resulted.

a. Identify at least four exposures for Southern Bend Ranch.

b.   Identify at least four exposures for Whole Organic Meat Market.

c.   For each exposure listed for Southern Bend Ranch, recommend at least one potential option.

d.   For each exposure listed for Whole Organic Meat Market, recommend at least one potential option.

Answers to Assignment 3 Questions

NOTE: These answers are provided to give students a basic understanding of acceptable types of responses. They often are not the only valid answers and are not intended to provide an exhaustive response to the questions.

Educational Objective 1

1-1. BCM involves examining potential threats to operations (such as natural disasters, building damage, or loss of a critical supplier) and establishing an operational plan with contingencies that allow the organization's key operations and critical functions to continue should such a disruption occur. BCM helps organizations withstand disruptive events and, ultimately, survive. BCM seeks to minimize the loss of resources essential to an organization's recovery from a disruption in operations. This is accomplished by focusing an organization's efforts on effective pre- and post-loss actions.

1-2. Risk management and BCM are similar in that they both involve planning, organizing, leading, and controlling an organization's resources and activities to achieve a particular result. However, BCM deals primarily with consequences of disruption; its focus on minimizing the results of disruptions to operations means it typically deals with operational risk. In contrast, risk management focuses more broadly on ongoing risk assessment and risk treatment and deals not only with operational risk, but also with hazard risk (property, liability, and personnel loss exposures), financial risk (resulting from the effect of market forces on financial assets or liabilities), and strategic risk (resulting from economic and societal trends).

1-3. The standards seek to encourage more U.S. organizations to prepare for emergencies. They provide organizations with guidelines for assessing their preparedness for hazards and for developing plans to protect their employees and to ensure recovery and continuity following disasters or other emergencies.

Educational Objective 2

2-1. The development of a business continuity plan allows an organization to analyze all possible eventualities to determine the critical functions that must continue during a disruption so that the organization survives, recovers, and resumes growth.

2-2. A BIA assesses what events may occur, when they may occur, and how they could affect achievement of the organization's key objectives. The BIA also measures the financial and nonfinancial effect of risks and explores organizational vulnerabilities, critical elements in developing strategies to protect organizational resources. By distinguishing between critical and noncritical processes, the BIA also allows the organization to determine its recovery time objective.

2-3. These models are used in continuity planning:

  a. Active backup model—The organization establishes a second site that includes all of the necessary production equipment housed at the primary site. Staff may be relocated to the second site if operations are disrupted at the primary site.

  b. Split operations model—The organization maintains two or more active sites that are geographically dispersed. Capacity at each site is sufficient to handle total output in the event of a disruption at either site.

    c.   Alternative site model—The organization maintains a production site and an active backup site that functions as the primary site as needed.

    d.   Contingency model—The organization develops an alternate way to maintain production, perhaps using manual processes.

2-4. Senior management provides the vision statement and support for the BCP and sets expectations and objectives for middle managers.

Educational Objective 3

3-1. The four stages of a strategic redeployment plan are these:

- Emergency stage
- Alternate marketing stage
- Contingency production stage
- Communication stage

3-2. The three objectives of the emergency stage of a strategic redeployment plan are these:

- Protect people—For example, by contacting emergency authorities, evacuating the area, and warning neighbors
- Protect physical assets—For example, by guarding the site and organizing salvage operations
- Protect reputation—For example, by communicating with all economic stakeholders and maintaining control of all media releases

3-3. The alternate marketing stage of strategic redeployment requires the organization to evaluate the impact of the disruption on the organization's reputation and market share. The organization must determine whether it needs a new marketing strategy. It must also consider consumer loyalty, the willingness of suppliers and subcontractors to work with the organization during this interval, and the potential for competitors to use the disruption as an opportunity to increase their market share or capture the affected organization's current suppliers.

3-4. At the contingency production stage, any downtime for the organization must be minimized. The organization must decide what products or services it will provide, depending on the facilities available and whether its technology and machinery are adequate. It must also consider its supply chain with respect to the quality and cost of resources needed and determine whether the product packaging must be adapted for a new product. Other considerations during this stage include the availability of transportation and of routes to distribute products and services.

3-5. The sole objective of the communication stage is to preserve or enhance stakeholders' trust and confidence in the organization.

Educational Objective 4

4-1. Supply chain risk management entails assessing and mitigating all the risks that might interrupt the normal flow of goods and services from and to an organization's stakeholders. When applied to the production of goods, supply chain risk management encompasses managing the volatility related to producing, transporting, and storing goods, as well as managing the distribution channels from the initial raw materials to the final consumer product. When applied to services, supply chain risk management encompasses managing the volatility associated with delivering the service to its end users, taking into consideration all the components of the value chain.

4-2. Internal supply chain exposures and vulnerabilities include these:

- Production location—Facilities may be vulnerable to natural disaster, manmade disaster, or terrorism.

- Production bottlenecks—Production may depend on a key machine or material; a malfunction or breakdown in the machine could slow or halt production.

- Information technology—The data center may be vulnerable, information backup may be unavailable, or staff may fail to follow restoration protocols.

- Infrastructure—Damage to infrastructure can impede or halt production altogether.

- Strikes or other employment issues—Production may cease, inventory cannot be moved, and orders are not filled.

- Machinery breakdown—Production may stall, or a critical backup in production may occur, while new parts (or new machines) are ordered and installed.

4-3.   External supply chain exposures and vulnerabilities include these:

- Third-party suppliers—Disruption in production from the supplier could undermine an organization's ability to generate its product and to satisfy customer demand.

- Sole source suppliers—Disruption in supply when only one supplier of goods is available will reduce or potentially shut down an organization's ability to produce and satisfy customer demand.

- Single source supplier—Disruptions in supply can also occur when an organization chooses to rely on only one supplier, even when multiple suppliers are available.

- Change in demand level—Incremental or substantial changes in demand because of changes in customer taste or to competition can cause over- or underproduction. If demand is not accurately forecasted, market reputation could be damaged.

- Financial risks—Increases in the cost of materials or transportation charges will cause costs to rise. Organizations may not be able to pass on increased costs because of consumer preferences, prior contracts, and competition. Exchange rate fluctuations may cause increases in material costs and may also reduce the attractiveness of the product in overseas markets.

- Geopolitical environment—Imports and exports may be affected by government regulation or taxation. Unstable governments increase the risk of nationalization of an organization's overseas assets.

- Natural or manmade catastrophes—Storms, earthquakes, volcanic eruptions, and other natural disasters can damage an organization's facilities or interfere with its transportation routes. Pandemics may interrupt an organization's activities if too few employees are available to work. Terrorist activity can disrupt normal supply and distribution channels for extended periods.

- Merger of a key supplier with a competitor—Changes in ownership of key suppliers can affect the price of materials and the availability of supplies.

4-4.   To establish supply chain best practices, an organization should have a multidisciplinary team of managers periodically assess its supply chain, prioritize potential risks, and determine disruption timing and recovery time. As it analyzes each type of disruption, the team should consider various responses, depending on the likelihood and impact of the potential disruption. Based on this review, the team should establish best practices, such as regularly using dry-running and updating the business continuity plan as conditions change.

Educational Objective 5

5-1. A good plan for stakeholder crisis communications includes several attributes:

- To be effective in restoring and maintaining stakeholders' trust after a crisis, the organization's message must be candid, address the prominent issues, and engage all stakeholders.

- The organization should maintain an open dialogue with the news media.

- Communication should effectively convey to various stakeholders that the organization has considered all risks.

- A theme emphasizing corporate involvement in safety and security should underlie the message.

- Communications must demonstrate that senior management is committed to maintaining an environment of transparency in its decision making.

- Crisis communications must be consistent and tailored to specific audiences.

- To maintain stakeholders' trust in the organization and its management, the messages must embody corporate integrity and authenticity.

5-2. Crisis communication specifically for internal stakeholders should cover these areas:

- Internal stakeholders' individual needs must be acknowledged.

- Employees must be informed continuously, especially regarding how the crisis will affect their jobs and working conditions.

- Any new safety concerns that emerge must be addressed. This can be done through meetings, displays of visual aids in the workplace, hands-on training, and the organization's intranet site.

- Unit and operational managers must be made aware of ongoing risks.

- Stockholders must be informed of all steps taken to manage, mitigate, and prevent future crises.

- Communicating organizational health in the annual report and during quarterly meetings is imperative. Senior management must report major trends and pending claims as well as demonstrate corporate resilience.

- The board of directors must be informed regularly about strategic exposures, governance issues, and long-term resilience.

5-3. Crisis communication specifically for external stakeholders should cover these areas:

- Suppliers must be notified of procedures for scheduled deliveries during the period of disruption and of how the organization will make required payments.

- Customers should be assured of the organization's continuity and safety. A sound communication plan can help build trust and maintain consumer loyalty during the period of recovery.

- Public officials and local authorities must be informed of the organization's efforts to ensure public safety and health and to demonstrate its commitment to the community.

- Statutory compliance must be monitored and reported.

- Local associations and special interest groups should be informed of the organization's recuperation efforts immediately after a crisis and as part of an ongoing effort to maintain strong relationships with these groups.

- News releases and interviews can be used to transmit information to both internal and external stakeholders.

- Every communication from the organization must be truthful. Risk professionals must speak clearly and honestly about current conditions, known risks, and potential risks.

Educational Objective 6

6-1. These answers relate to the Southern Bend Ranch case.

a. Southern Bend Ranch has these exposures (among others):

- Whole Organic may sue Southern Bend Ranch for failure to honor the contract terms related to the amount of meat supplied.

- The flooding has caused a decrease in production.

- Southern Bend's reputation may be damaged because of its inability to honor the contract with Whole Organic and to meet its other customers' demands.

- Southern Bend may consider suing the quasi-governmental agency for its failure to anticipate the flooding. (Depending on the outcome of the lawsuit, this could result in either a loss or a gain to Southern Bend.)

b. Examples of exposures for Whole Organic Meat Market include these:

- It may lose market share because it no longer has sufficient meat to meet demand.

- Southern Bend is Whole Organic's only supplier of meat; Whole Organic may not be able to get high-quality organic meat elsewhere.

- Whole Organic may sue Southern Bend Ranch for breach of contract (which, depending on the outcome of the suit, could result in either a loss or a gain).

- Its reputation may be damaged, and it may lose customers because it cannot meet their demand for the meat.

c. The potential options for the exposures include these:

- Whole Organic's lawsuit—Communicate/mediate with Whole Organic to avoid the lawsuit; renegotiate contracts to clarify "acts of God" provisions

- Decrease in production because of flood—Consolidate herds; buy more organic grain and increase grain feed to compensate for reduced availability of grass

- Reputation/customer loyalty—Communicate with customers about the cause of the decrease in beef and venison supplies

- Possible litigation against quasi-governmental entity—Investigate possibility that Southern Bend Ranch could recover some of its losses from the agency that was responsible for the flooding

d. The potential options for the exposures include these:

- Loss of market share—Increase supplies of chicken, pork, and emu to compensate for the reduction of beef and venison supplies

- Limited number of organic meat suppliers—Investigate other suppliers, even if they must ship from out of state

- Litigation (suing Southern Bend Ranch)—Resolve issues; renegotiate contracts; negotiate a settlement

- Loss of reputation and customers—Buy more organic chicken, pork, and emu from suppliers; run specials on these meats to increase sales; advertise specials and communicate with customers

Direct Your Learning

Physical Property Risk

Educational Objectives

After learning the content of this assignment, you should be able to:

1. Describe various categories of physical property exposed to risk.

2. Describe the major sources of risk affecting physical property.

3. Describe the nature of and the pre-loss and post-loss actions appropriate for windstorms, earthquakes, and floods.

4. Explain how a building's construction and occupancy reduce the likelihood and consequences of fire damage.

5. Explain how a building's protection and external exposures reduce the likelihood and consequences of fire damage.

6. Explain how human characteristics, building occupancies, and the Life Safety Code affect the safety of persons exposed to fire in buildings.

7. Explain how to use various methods to value physical property.

8. Describe the types of legal interests in physical property.

9. Given information on a physical property, assess the risk and recommend treatment options for protecting lives and property.

Outline

- ▶ **Physical Property Categories**
  - A. Real Property
    1. Land
    2. Buildings and Other Structures
  - B. Tangible Personal Property
- ▶ **Sources of Property Risk**
  - A. Natural Risk Sources
    1. Windstorm
    2. Earthquake
    3. Flood
    4. Fire and Lightning
    5. Smoke
    6. Water
  - B. Human Risk Sources
    1. Riot and Civil Commotion
    2. Explosion
    3. Vandalism
    4. Vehicles
    5. Collapse
    6. Crime
  - C. Economic Risk Sources
- ▶ **Windstorm, Earthquake, and Flood Loss Control**
  - A. Windstorm
    1. Pre-Loss Actions for Windstorm
    2. Post-Loss Actions for Windstorm
  - B. Tornado
    1. Pre-Loss Actions for Tornadoes
    2. Post-Loss Actions for Tornadoes
  - C. Earthquake
    1. Pre-Loss Actions for Earthquake
    2. Post-Loss Actions for Earthquake
  - D. Flood
    1. Pre-Loss Actions for Flood
    2. Post-Loss Actions for Flood

- ▶ **Building Construction and Occupancy**
  - A. Construction
    1. Frame
    2. Joisted Masonry
    3. Noncombustible
    4. Modified Fire-Resistive
    5. Fire-Resistive
    6. Fire Divisions
  - B. Occupancy
    1. Habitational
    2. Office
    3. Institutional
    4. Mercantile
    5. Service
    6. Manufacturers
- ▶ **Building Protection and External Exposures**
  - A. Internal Fire Protection
    1. Detection
    2. Suppression
  - B. External Fire Protection
  - C. Exterior Environment
    1. Evaluating Exterior Exposures
    2. Controlling Exterior Exposures
- ▶ **Life Safety**
  - A. Human Characteristics
  - B. Building Occupancies
  - C. Life Safety Code
- ▶ **Valuing Physical Property**
  - A. Book Value
  - B. Replacement Cost
    1. Buildings
    2. Personal Property
    3. Functional Replacement Cost
  - C. Market Value
  - D. Economic Value

s.m.a.r.t. tips

Use the SMART Online Practice Exams to test your understanding of the course material. You can review questions over a single assignment or multiple assignments, or you can take an exam over the entire course.

▶▶

Outline

▶ **Legal Interests in Physical Property**
   A. Ownership Interest
   B. Secured Creditor's Interest
   C. Seller's and Buyer's Interest
   D. Bailee's Interest
   E. Landlord's Interest
   F. Tenant's Interest

▶ **Assessing and Treating Physical Property Risk**
   A. Case Facts
   B. Overview of Steps
   C. Risk Assessment
   D. Risk Treatment

For each assignment, you should define or describe each of the Key Words and Phrases and answer each of the Review and Application Questions.

Educational Objective 1
Describe various categories of physical property exposed to risk.

Key Words and Phrases

Real property (realty)

Tangible property

Intangible property

Review Questions

1-1. Identify attributes of unimproved land that may make it difficult to value.

1-2. List the different types of buildings and other structures that are permanent improvements when added to real property.

▶▶

1-3. Describe these categories of tangible property and the issues a risk management professional needs to consider with each:

    a. Money and securities

    b. Accounts receivable records

    c. Inventory

    d. Furniture, equipment, or supplies

    e. Computer equipment and media

    f.   Machinery

    g.   Valuable papers and records

    h.   Mobile property

Educational Objective 2
Describe the major sources of risk affecting physical property.

Key Words and Phrases
Windstorm

Earthquake focus

Epicenter

▶▶

Modified Mercalli Intensity Scale

Terrorism

Review Questions

2-1. Explain how risk management can address natural risk sources.

2-2. Describe the types of windstorms that can cause significant damage.

2-3. Describe the two measures of earthquakes.

2-4. Identify the seven common types of floods.

2-5. Describe the types of water sources that may cause water damage to structures.

2-6. Identify the types of damage that typically result from rioting.

2-7. Describe the types of losses that can result from acts of terrorism.

Application Question

2-8. Major Retailer has locations throughout Florida and is subject to many sources of property risk.

a. Identify three natural risk sources to which Major Retailer may be susceptible.

b. Identify the economic risk sources to which Major Retailer may be susceptible.

Educational Objective 3
Describe the nature of and the pre-loss and post-loss actions appropriate for windstorms, earthquakes, and floods.

Key Words and Phrases
Tornado

Box action design

Frame action design

Review Questions

3-1.   Describe the pre-loss disaster recovery actions for windstorm.

3-2.   Describe the post-loss disaster recovery actions that may help to reduce further damage to buildings and equipment.

3-3.   Describe the post-loss disaster recovery procedures for tornadoes.

3-4.   Explain why location is a key factor in controlling earthquake damage to property and injuries to people.

3-5. Identify the two areas of focus for post-loss disaster recovery actions following an earthquake.

3-6. Describe the cause of tsunamis and tidal waves.

3-7. Describe the pre-loss disaster recovery actions for minimizing fire loss exposures resulting from flooding.

Application Question

3-8. A Japanese car manufacturer is considering opening an assembly plant in the central United States. Having seen the devastation a tornado can cause in this area, the managers of the manufacturer are particularly concerned about that risk source. Their concern is not just about the physical plant but also about the personnel in the plant in the event of a tornado.

Describe the pre-loss actions for tornadoes that the car manufacturer should consider in planning this new location.

Educational Objective 4

Explain how a building's construction and occupancy reduce the likelihood and consequences of fire damage.

Key Words and Phrases

Frame construction

Joisted masonry construction

Heavy timber construction (mill construction)

Noncombustible construction

Masonry noncombustible construction

Modified fire-resistive construction

Fire-resistive construction

Fire division

Fender wall

Ignition source

Review Questions

4-1. Identify the distinguishing characteristics of each of the following types of building construction:

a. Frame

b. Joisted masonry

c. Heavy timber

4-2. Contrast noncombustible construction with masonry noncombustible construction.

4-3. Describe the operation of fire divisions.

4-4. Explain why controlling the threat of hostile fires in habitational occupancies is difficult.

4-5. Identify the common ignition sources found in habitational occupancies.

4-6. Describe the primary ignition sources for office occupancies.

Application Question

4-7. A large department store chain wants to construct a distribution center in the southern United States that will serve as a regional warehouse for a two-hundred-mile radius. Warehouse managers have informed the chain's risk management professional that under normal circumstances of staffing, availability of moving equipment, amount of inventory, and depending on where a fire originates, it will probably take one hour to evacuate 60 percent of the value of the inventory. Sixty percent is the target set by the chief financial officer, based on her level of risk tolerance. Recognizing that the cost of construction typically rises as a more fire-resistive type of construction is chosen, recommend the least expensive building construction type that will still allow the warehouse personnel to meet their 60 percent target under normal circumstances and explain why each less expensive construction type would be inappropriate.

Educational Objective 5

Explain how a building's protection and external exposures reduce the likelihood and consequences of fire damage.

Key Words and Phrases

Internal (or private) fire protection

External (or public) fire protection

Automatic fire suppression system

Sprinkler system

Wet pipe sprinkler systems

Dry pipe sprinkler systems

Deluge system

Preaction sprinkler system

Dry chemical system

Carbon dioxide system

Gas extinguishing system

Foam system

Standpipe system

Review Questions

5-1.   Identify the two integral parts of a fire suppression system.

5-2.   Identify the five basic types of fire alarms.

5-3.   Describe the components of an automatic fire suppression system.

5-4.   Contrast the uses of deluge sprinkler systems with those of preaction sprinkler systems.

5-5.   Describe the operation of foam sprinkler systems.

5-6. Explain why it is important for employees to be trained to use fire extinguishers.

5-7. Describe the factors that influence the effectiveness of external fire protection.

5-8. List the factors that a risk management professional should consider when working with a public fire department.

5-9. Explain why it is important to control exterior exposures by keeping the area between buildings clear.

5-10. Explain how a water-spray system can help to prevent the spread of fire from one building to a neighboring building.

Application Question

5-11. An insurance agency is located in a two-story masonry building. The building located next door to the agency is a twelve-story masonry apartment building that includes balconies and large bay windows on all sides.

Describe the construction considerations that would influence the spread of fire from the apartment building to the insurance agency's building.

Educational Objective 6

Explain how human characteristics, building occupancies, and the Life Safety Code affect the safety of persons exposed to fire in buildings.

Key Words and Phrases

Fire safety

Life safety

Review Questions

6-1. List the four human characteristics that affect susceptibility to injury or death of individuals caused by a building fire.

6-2. Describe the life safety concerns related to day care building occupancies.

6-3. Describe the life safety concerns related to detention and correctional building occupancies.

6-4. Explain the importance of complying with the Life Safety Code.

Application Question

6-5. A shopping mall that takes up an entire city block includes a movie theater and several bar/restaurant operations. On a Friday night at 7:00 p.m., a fire occurs in the kitchen of one of the restaurants. Smoke spreads rapidly through the mall, causing fire alarms to sound throughout the building. Explain how the characteristics affecting classes of occupancies and building occupants' susceptibility to fire apply to these groups of patrons.

    a.   Young children in the movie theater, which is currently showing a film that appeals primarily to an audience under twelve years of age.

b.   Shoppers in a department store within the mall.

c.   Customers at a bar/restaurant featuring a "happy hour" event from 5:30 to 7:30 p.m.

Educational Objective 7
Explain how to use various methods to value physical property.

Key Words and Phrases

Book value (net depreciated value)

Historical cost

Replacement cost

Functional replacement cost

Market value

Economic value

Review Questions

7-1. Identify the typical approaches to valuing property.

7-2. Explain why risk management professionals do not rely on the book value of a property.

7-3. Explain the circumstances in which a risk management professional may choose functional replacement cost as a means of valuing property.

7-4. Explain the circumstances in which a risk management professional may choose market value as a means of valuing property.

7-5. Explain when economic value would be used for risk management purposes.

Application Question

7-6. Childrens' Hospital was built two years ago on property donated by a philan-thropist. The former home of the philanthropist, a fifty-room mansion, is now part of the hospital and is used as offices. What approaches might the hospital's risk management professional use to value its property?

Educational Objective 8

Describe the types of legal interests in physical property.

Key Words and Phrases

Secured creditor

Bailee

Bailor

Bailment contract

Trade fixtures

Review Questions

8-1. Identify the categories of legal interests in physical property.

8-2. Describe two ways a common carrier's liability may be limited.

8-3. Describe the legal interests of tenants regarding these:

    a.   Improvements and betterments

    b.   Trade fixtures

Application Question

8-4. Grocery Store operates its business from a building owned by Leasing Company. Grocery Store has made numerous improvements to the building, including permanent walls that separate the retail section of the store from the storage section of the store. Grocery Store has also added merchandise shelves (called gondolas) that form the aisles of the store. What responsibility, if any, would Leasing Company have to Grocery Store for damages to Grocery Store's improvements?

Educational Objective 9

Given information on a physical property, assess the risk and recommend treatment options for protecting lives and property.

Application Question

9-1. You are the risk manager for a resort hotel operation in California. The hotel has 380 rooms, two restaurants, two swimming pools, several retail stores, and a golf course.

   a. Describe the tangible personal property you as the risk manager might identify as part of the risk assessment process.

b. Describe the natural and economic risk sources affecting physical property at this location.

c. Describe the types of internal fire protection risk control measures that could be used to reduce the likelihood and consequences of fire damage at this hotel.

Answers to Assignment 4 Questions

NOTE: These answers are provided to give students a basic understanding of acceptable types of responses. They often are not the only valid answers and are not intended to provide an exhaustive response to the questions.

Educational Objective 1

1-1. Attributes of unimproved land that may make it difficult to value include water, mineral resources, natural attractions of commercial value, natural forests, and resident wild animals.

1-2. Examples of buildings and other structures that are permanent improvements when added to real property include:

- Buildings: homes (including trailers on cement slabs), churches, schools, stores, factories, and offices

- Outbuildings: sheds, barns, stables, and greenhouses

- Other structures: hookups to sewer and electrical facilities, roads, fences, and retaining walls

1-3. These answers describe categories of tangible property and the issues a risk management professional needs to consider with each:

a. Money and securities—Includes cash, bank accounts, certificates of deposit, securities, notes, drafts, and evidence of debt. The risk management professional needs to consider an organization's cash on hand, large embezzlement losses over time, and the possibility of theft by either employees or outsiders.

b. Accounts receivable records—Records that show the money currently due and previously collected from customer or client accounts. The risk management professional needs to consider an organization's data backup and offsite storage.

c. Inventory—Includes goods ready for sale, raw materials, stock in process, and finished goods. The risk management professional needs to consider the fluctuating values at different production stages and the wide range of causes of loss.

d. Furniture, equipment, or supplies—Includes office furniture, showcases, counters, office and manufacturing supplies, and packaging materials. The risk management professional needs to consider the organization's ownership of supplies and of expensive or specialized equipment that cannot be easily replaced.

e. Computer equipment and media—Includes computers and other data-processing hardware, software, data, and specialized environmental control systems. The risk management professional needs to consider physical damage causes of loss, including damage from excessive heat or moisture. Computers may also be damaged by electrical impulses or power surges. Also, computer fraud by employees or outsiders sometimes involves theft of property. Alternatively, an employee or outsider may try to sabotage computer equipment.

f. Machinery—Includes equipment that may or may not be computer controlled. The risk management professional needs to consider the significant value of this equipment.

g.   Valuable papers and records—Includes medical histories of patients, project reference files, and physical documents associated with intangible property, such as deeds and films. The risk management professional needs to consider the organization's method of safekeeping and the valuation of these papers and records.

h.   Mobile property—Includes autos, aircraft, boats, ships, and heavy mobile equipment. The risk management professional needs to consider the large values of some items and the special hazards associated with them.

Educational Objective 2

2-1.   The occurrence of a natural risk source is largely beyond human control. Consequently, risk management has little, if any, effect on reducing the likelihood of an event. However, organizations can implement loss reduction measures to control the consequences of any events.

2-2.   These types of windstorms can cause damage:

- Hurricane—a severe tropical cyclone, usually accompanied by heavy rains and winds of seventy-five miles per hour or more.

- Tornado—a localized and violently destructive windstorm occurring over land and characterized by a funnel-shaped cloud extending toward the ground. A tornado consists of winds rotating at speeds up to 300 miles per hour. Winter storms can also be a significant source of catastrophic losses.

2-3.   The two measures of earthquakes are the Richter scale and the Modified Mercalli Intensity Scale. Seismologists use the Richter scale to measure, by either magnitude or intensity, the energy released by an earthquake at its epicenter. The Modified Mercalli Intensity Scale measures intensity—the damage that an earthquake causes to people, property, and the surface of the earth—rather than magnitude.

2-4.   These are the seven common types of floods:

- Riverine floods, which occur when rivers or streams overflow their banks.

- Tidal floods, which result from high tides, frequently driven by high winds offshore, and from tropical storms making landfall or passing closely offshore.

- Wind floods can happen whenever a strong wind holds back part of a large body of water from its normal drainage course and raises the water level.

- Rising water levels downstream might prevent drainage upstream, causing a backwater flood.

- Ice jams sometimes develop as ice thaws and begins to move downstream. They block the flow of water, causing it to back up and flood upstream areas.

- Accidental floods are caused by the failure of flood control systems.

- Man-made topographic changes can also cause floods. For example, instead of being absorbed into the soil, rain water can accumulate on concrete and asphalt parking lots.

2-5.   Water damage can occur when a pipe bursts; when a fracture develops in an appliance, thereby allowing water seepage; and when sewer systems back up through toilets, sinks, and drains. Many commercial structures are protected by sprinkler systems, which can leak if not properly maintained or if damaged.

2-6. Types of damage that typically result from rioting include fire, breakage, theft, looting, and vandalism.

2-7. Terrorism may involve the deliberate contamination of property through chemical, biological, or radioactive materials, or the destruction of property by bombing or aerial impact.

2-8. These answers apply to Major Retailer:

a. Because Major Retailer has locations throughout Florida, it is susceptible to various natural risk sources, such as windstorm, hurricanes, and flooding. Additionally, Major Retailer is subject to fire and lightning, smoke, and water damage such as sprinkler leakage.

b. Major Retailer may be subject to economic risk sources such as changes in price levels, interest rates, the general economy, or consumer preferences.

Educational Objective 3

3-1. Pre-loss actions for windstorm include these:

- Design buildings and outside structures to withstand anticipated wind loads. The design should reflect location conditions in which wind velocities might exceed the average.

- Provide storm shutters and blinds for windows and other openings rated to handle higher wind loads.

- Maintain roof and wall systems, including roof tie-downs, in good repair and provide adequate supports for outside structures.

- Secure materials and equipment located in areas surrounding the facility.

3-2. Spare construction materials, such as plywood panels, tarpaulins, and plastic sheets can be used to temporarily repair damage to buildings and to reduce further damage to the building and equipment exposed to the elements.

3-3. These are appropriate post-tornado procedures:

- Begin search and rescue process

- Complete temporary repairs to avoid additional property damage

- Proceed with caution near downed power lines

- Start salvage procedures

3-4. First, people and property located farther away from volcanic areas and major geological faults (where earthquakes tend to concentrate) are less likely to experience detectable earthquakes than those located nearer to such areas. Second, at any given distance from an epicenter, people and structures situated on stable earth that can absorb most earthquake shock waves tend to suffer less harm than those located on more unstable ground.

3-5. Immediate post-loss actions following an earthquake should focus on these areas:

- Take care of both injured and noninjured people

- Take any possible actions to protect damaged buildings and infrastructure from further damage

3-6. Oceanic seismic activity can cause a tsunami or tidal wave, which can travel at up to 600 miles per hour in deep water. As a tidal wave enters the coastal shoals, its velocity is greatly reduced, but its wave height increases. Some tidal waves can crest at over 100 feet.

3-7. Pre-loss actions for minimizing fire loss exposures resulting from floods include these:

- Allow no open flames or electrical wiring that is not waterproof near or in a flood-exposed structure

- Protect flammable gas piping (whether utility or process services) where exposed to mechanical damage and install shutoffs or disconnects above normally expected flood stage heights

- Prevent flood water from entering buildings, either by having no lower-level openings or by covering those openings against water entry

3-8. The company should consider where the plant will be located, as some central U.S. states have a higher frequency of tornado activity than other states. It is difficult to prevent damage to the physical plant from tornadoes, however, some reinforced concrete construction has withstood tornado-force winds and should be considered in the building design. To reduce injury to plant personnel, underground shelters should be installed to provide a safe place of evacuation in the event of a tornado.

Educational Objective 4

4-1. These answers refer to questions regarding the distinguishing characteristics of types of building construction:

a. Exterior walls are made either of combustible material (such as wood) or a noncombustible material (such as brick veneer). Wall supports, floors, and roof are made of combustible material.

b. Exterior walls are made of masonry (such as brick, stone, concrete, or hollow concrete block or other noncombustible materials). Other structural components, such as the floors and roof, are usually made of combustible materials.

c. Involves heavy timber structural supports and masonry wall construction.

4-2. Noncombustible constructions include buildings with exterior walls, floors, and roof made of and supported by noncombustible materials but with trim and interior walls that may be made of combustible materials. Masonry noncombustible construction includes buildings with exterior walls made of masonry or of fire-resistive materials with a fire resistive rating of not less than one hour, and floors and roof made of noncombustible materials with noncombustible supports.

4-3. A well-designed fire division prevents a fire originating outside the division from spreading into the division. Fire can spread both horizontally and vertically. A vertical opening, such as an elevator or a stairwell, is protected when segregated into a separate fire division. Fire divisions can also restrict the spread of fire in large horizontal structures by separating areas either by two independent walls or by one continuous, common masonry wall that divides two adjoining properties.

4-4. Habitational occupancies are often in the control of someone other than the building owner, so detecting or controlling hazards can be difficult.

▶▶

4-5. Common ignition sources in habitational occupancies include cooking equipment, overheated machinery and equipment (for example, clothes dryers, from which fires can spread rapidly because of lint accumulation), malfunctioning appliances, and faulty wiring (electrical equipment).

4-6. The primary ignition sources for fires that originate in office occupancies are faulty or malfunctioning wiring and electrical and lighting equipment.

4-7. The risk management professional should recommend the building construction type of modified fire-resistive. This construction type requires construction design and materials that will maintain structural integrity despite exposure to fire for between one and two hours. Although likely less expensive, frame construction is inappropriate because it has wall supports, floors, and roofs that are combustible and cannot be relied on to maintain the structural integrity needed to remove the inventory. Joisted masonry construction has noncombustible wall supports, but the floors and walls are still combustible and therefore inappropriate. Noncombustible construction and masonry noncombustible may be appropriate types of construction with their exterior walls, floors, and roofs made of noncombustible materials. However, only the exterior walls (not including the floor or roof) of the masonry noncombustible type is rated for at least an hour and, as stated, one hour (enough time to save 60 percent of inventory) is the minimum required by the CFO. Fire-resistive construction would also provide the needed fire protection but would likely cost more to construct than masonry noncombustible and therefore is not as desirable.

Educational Objective 5

5-1. Two integral parts of every suppression system are fire detection devices to activate the system and alarm devices to alert an outside fire department or the organization's personnel.

5-2. The five basic types of fire alarms, in terms of where the alarm signal is received, are local alarms, auxiliary alarms, remote alarms, proprietary alarms, and central station alarms.

5-3. Automatic fire suppression systems consist of piping with discharging nozzles or heads, control valves for directing extinguishing agents within the system, gauges for monitoring pressure within the system, and alarm devices to signal when the system becomes operative. Some systems also have other monitoring alarms that signal malfunction so that the systems can be repaired.

5-4. Deluge sprinkler systems are used to protect against fires that could quickly spread, such as spills of flammable liquids. Preaction systems are particularly appropriate for occupancies that are especially susceptible to water damage, such as computer rooms or libraries.

5-5. Foam systems extinguish fires by smothering them with a foam blanket and separating the fuel from the air (oxygen). The foam blanket also suppresses the release of flammable vapors that can mix with the air. A foam system requires proportioning equipment to mix the foam with water in the required concentration.

5-6. As education is an important part of risk control, employees should be trained to use fire extinguishers. Education includes training on extinguishers' locations, their discharge ranges, their capabilities and limitations, and their methods of use. For some highly hazardous operations, personnel should have on-the-spot extinguisher training in a controlled-fire setting.

5-7. External fire protection is effective only when adequate services and equipment are available. This means public fire hydrants are reasonably accessible, the hydrants have adequate water volume and pressure, the fire department has appropriate firefighting equipment, and fire department personnel are trained and capable of responding to a fire at a facility.

5-8. When working with a public fire department, a risk management professional should consider these factors:

- The distance from the fire department to the organization's property

- The terrain and obstructions that might interfere with the fire department's response (for example, hilly roads, railroad tracks, roads with rush hour traffic, or road areas that might be subject to flooding or other natural causes of loss)

- The time it takes for the fire department to respond to a fire

5-9. If a wall or fence obstructs the area around a building, it is difficult for firefighters to position hoses so that water reaches the building. If the area is covered with brush, combustible trash, or stacks of pallets of waste paper, a ready fuel source is created that can rapidly spread fire. Removing this material slows the spread of fire.

5-10. A water-spray system can help to prevent the spread of fire from one building to a neighboring building, as it has open, directional spray nozzles to soak an exposed building. When used for protection, water-spray systems are usually activated manually.

5-11. When evaluating the exterior external exposures of the insurance agency, a risk management professional should consider these construction components:

- Building materials influence fire frequency and severity. The chance of a fire spreading from the joisted masonry apartment building is greater than from a fire-resistive building.

- Building height and area also increase the fire hazard. Because the apartment building is twelve stories, more intense fires may develop and firefighters may have more difficulty reaching higher floors and containing a fire.

- Wall openings also increase the chance that fire will spread from one building to another. Because the wall facing the insurance agency has balconies and windows, fire and heat can radiate from the apartment building.

Educational Objective 6

6-1. The four human characteristics that affect susceptibility to injury or death of individuals caused by a building fire are age, mobility, awareness of the fire, and knowledge of the building.

6-2. Day care occupancies contain both young and senior occupants who are supervised by adults other than their relatives or legal guardians.

6-3. Detention and correctional building occupancies house occupants that are incapable of self-preservation because of imposed security.

6-4. Compliance with applicable provisions of the Life Safety Code is usually a legal requirement. Failing to comply is not only a breach of an ordinance (resulting in fines and other penalties) but can also indicate negligence in failing to adequately safeguard others. Consequently, not complying with the Life Safety Code increases the likelihood not only of property and personnel losses but also of liability losses.

6-5. These answers apply to questions regarding the shopping mall fire:

   a. The theater is an assembly occupancy that generally contains large numbers of people who are unfamiliar with the spaces. Young children are usually less mobile and less aware of a fire. The children may not understand the purpose of the fire alarm warning and may also be distracted by the movie.

   b. Retail stores contain large numbers of people in a space that is relatively unfamiliar to them and may also contain a large amount of combustible contents. The occupants are likely to include all ages, but most should have good mobility. Their distraction level should be relatively low and most should be able to detect the fire once the smoke or fire alarm becomes evident. The knowledge of the building would differ based on whether shoppers were new to the store or had shopped there previously. Most occupants would need assistance in locating a fire exit from store or mall employees.

   c. These customers would be of drinking age and therefore old enough to be mobile and aware of a fire. However, their mobility may be affected by alcohol, and some may need assistance to quickly evacuate the building. Alcohol consumption may also impair their knowledge of the building and affect discipline and control of the occupants.

Educational Objective 7

7-1. These are some of the typical approaches to valuing property:

   - Book value

   - Replacement cost

   - Market value

   - Economic value

7-2. A long-term asset's book value is lower than its market value because inflation increases the market value while depreciation decreases the book value.

7-3. A risk management professional may choose functional replacement cost as a means of valuing property that is easily affected by technological changes.

7-4. A risk management professional may choose market value as a means of valuing products that are relatively indistinguishable from one another, such as agricultural products, oil, or precious metals. These nonspecialized products are considered commodities and are traded as such on organized exchanges. Consequently, these products have a determinable daily market value.

7-5. For risk management purposes, economic value can be relevant in measuring property risk exposures for real or personal property that the organization would not replace if it became damaged or destroyed. This is true because economic value focuses on the effect that the loss of the property would have on the organization's future income and, therefore, the property's contribution to the organization's overall value and net worth.

▶▶

7-6. Childrens' Hospital's risk management professional will likely choose to use several approaches to value its property. Because the hospital is only two years old, historical cost might be very accurate. As with historical cost, book value may offer a relevant value because of the hospital's newness. Replacement cost is likely the best approach, although it may take considerable research to determine. The fifty-room mansion would also be valued using replacement cost or functional replacement cost. Buildings such as this have little economic value but very high replacement costs because they include ornate features or were specifically designed for a use that is obsolete because of technological advances. Functional replacement cost may also be the best approach to valuing the hospital's personal property because much of it is technologically based. Economic value may be a consideration for the hospital, but other property valuation methods would likely be more useful.

Educational Objective 8

8-1. These are the categories of legal interests in physical property:

- Ownership interest

- Secured creditor's interest

- Seller's and buyer's interest

- Bailee's interest

- Landlord's interest

- Tenant's interest

8-2. A common carrier's liability may be limited in two ways: by statute or by the common carrier's bill of lading (the contract between the parties). If liability is not limited, a common carrier is responsible for the full value of the property transported.

8-3. These answers explain the legal interests of tenants:

a. Improvements and betterments are alterations to the premises that are intended to remain permanently attached to the building and that make the property more useful for the tenant's purpose. These alternations become part of the leased structure.

b. Trade fixtures are alterations to the premises that are not intended to remain permanently attached to the building. These alterations are usually treated as personal property and may be removed when the tenant leaves.

8-4. Leasing Company would not normally be responsible for the value of either the improvements and betterments (that is, the wall separating the retail section of the store and the storage section of the store) or the trade fixtures (that is, the gondolas). However, the lease between Leasing Company and Grocery Store may specify otherwise, and it would take precedence.

Educational Objective 9

9-1. These answers apply to questions regarding the hotel operation:

    a. The major type of personal property would be furniture, equipment, and supplies. This includes furnishings in the hotel rooms and public areas of the hotel as well as in offices, restaurants, and stores. All outdoor furnishings such as tables, chairs, and other furniture at the pool locations would be included in this category. All equipment used to maintain the property and grounds is considered tangible personal property. Other tangible personal property includes money and securities, accounts receivable records, and computers. Another important type of tangible property to be considered is any mobile property, which would include golf carts and other equipment such as backhoes, mowers, and tractors used for upkeep of the golf course.

    b. Natural risk sources include fire, lightning, and wind. Because this hotel is located in California, earthquake is one risk source of particular concern. Also, uncontrollable vegetation or drought conditions could significantly affect the golf course. Economic risk sources include changes in consumer preferences, recession, variations in levels of business and pleasure travel, and the overall condition of the general economy. These factors could positively or negatively affect this hotel operation.

    c. Internal fire protection consists of detection devices such as heat, smoke, and flame detectors and alarm devices to alert individuals on premises as well as signal a fire occurrence to outside fire departments. Suppression measures include sprinkler systems, fire extinguishers, and standpipe systems for the hotel and dry chemical systems to protect cooking operations in the restaurants.

B

Direct Your Learning

5

Intellectual Property and Reputation Risk

Educational Objectives

After learning the content of this assignment, you should be able to:

1. Describe the nature of and types of intellectual property protection.

2. Describe the features of copyrights and risk control measures for copyright loss exposures.

3. Describe the features of trademarks and risk control measures for trademark loss exposures.

4. Describe the features of patents and risk control measures for patent loss exposures.

5. Describe the features of trade secrets and risk control methods for trade secret loss exposures.

6. Describe the importance of and methods for valuing intellectual property.

7. Describe each of the following with regard to reputation risk:

   - Reputation as a key asset

   - Key risk sources

   - Systemic approach to managing reputation risk

   - Implementation of risk management for reputation risk

Outline

▶ **Introduction to Intellectual Property Risk**
  A. Nature of Intellectual Property Protection
  B. Types of Intellectual Property Protection

▶ **Copyrights**
  A. Copyright Features
    1. Copyright Creation
    2. Copyright Ownership
    3. Copyright Duration
  B. Risk Control Measures for Copyright Loss Exposures
    1. Notice
    2. Registration
    3. Restrictive Covenants
    4. Responses to Anticipated Defenses
    5. Licensing Agreements

▶ **Trademarks**
  A. Features of Trademarks
    1. Categories
    2. Creation
    3. Duration
  B. Risk Control Measures for Trademark Loss Exposures
    1. Notice
    2. Registration
    3. Searches and Watches
    4. Licensing Agreements
    5. Restrictive Covenants
    6. Enforcement of Rights

▶ **Patents**
  A. Features of Patents
  B. Risk Control Measures for Patent Loss Exposures

▶ **Trade Secrets**
  A. Features of Trade Secrets
  B. Trade Secret Loss Exposures
  C. Risk Control Measures for Trade Secret Loss Exposures

▶ **Valuing Intellectual Property**
  A. Reasons for Valuing Intellectual Property
  B. Valuation Methodologies

▶ **Reputation Risk**
  A. Reputation as a Key Asset
  B. Key Risk Sources
  C. Systemic Approach to Managing Reputation Risk
  D. Implementation of Risk Management for Reputation Risk

s.m.a.r.t. tips   When you take the randomized full practice exams in the SMART Online Practice Exams product, you are seeing the same kinds of questions you will see when you take the actual exam.

▶▶

For each assignment, you should define or describe each of the Key Words and Phrases and answer each of the Review and Application Questions.

Educational Objective 1
Describe the nature of and types of intellectual property protection.

Key Words and Phrases

Intellectual property

Infringement

Review Questions

1-1. Identify the source of intellectual property's value.

1-2. Identify the method intellectual property owners historically have used to enforce their rights.

1-3. Explain the significance of the Paris Convention to intellectual property rights.

1-4. Identify the intent of a trademark.

1-5. Define trade secret.

Educational Objective 2
Describe the features of copyrights and risk control measures for copyright loss exposures.

Key Words and Phrases
Work for hire

Laches

Review Questions

2-1. Identify the three important features of copyright.

2-2. Identify the three criteria a work must meet to be considered copyrighted.

2-3. Explain the importance of determining whether an organization or an organization's employee owns the copyright on a work the employee creates.

2-4. Identify examples of risk control measures that can be used for copyright loss exposures.

2-5. Identify two benefits associated with registering a copyright.

2-6. Define restrictive covenant.

Educational Objective 3
Describe the features of trademarks and risk control measures for trademark loss exposures.

Key Words and Phrases
Servicemark

Trade dress

Review Questions
3-1. Identify the purpose of a trademark.

3-2.   Identify three important features shared by trademarks, servicemarks, and trade dress.

3-3.   Identify the characteristic of an arbitrary mark that makes it memorable.

3-4.   Define fanciful mark.

3-5.   Identify risk control measures that may be used for trademark and servicemark loss exposures.

Educational Objective 4
Describe the features of patents and risk control measures for patent loss exposures.

Review Questions

4-1. Identify the three types of patents.

4-2. Identify the three characteristics that an invention must have to be eligible for a patent in the United States.

4-3. Explain the role of monitoring firms in the patent application process.

4-4. Identify the risk control measures that can be used for patent loss exposures.

Application Question

4-5. An organization's management determines that its intellectual property may be vulnerable to theft in the absence of an employment contract that addresses the topic. Describe the elements the contract should include to insure that the organization's employees cannot infringe on its intellectual property.

Educational Objective 5

Describe the features of trade secrets and risk control methods for trade secret loss exposures.

Key Word or Phrase

Reverse engineering

Review Questions

5-1. Identify the most obvious loss exposure associated with trade secrets.

5-2. Identify the starting point courts use to determine whether an invention, idea, or process qualifies as a trade secret.

5-3. Identify the questions courts answer to determine trade secret status.

5-4. Identify the risk control measures that can be used to ensure information confidentiality.

Educational Objective 6

Describe the importance of and methods for valuing intellectual property.

Review Questions

6-1. Identify examples of methods organizations can use to safeguard some of their intellectual property.

6-2. Identify why protecting all of an organization's intellectual property is challenging.

6-3. Explain the importance of accurately valued intellectual property in a situation in which an organization is faced with unauthorized use of its intellectual property.

6-4. Describe the most frequently used intellectual property valuation methodologies.

Educational Objective 7

Describe each of the following with regard to reputation risk:

- **Reputation as a key asset**
- **Key risk sources**
- **Systemic approach to managing reputation risk**
- **Implementation of risk management for reputation risk**

Key Word or Phrase

Reputation

Review Questions

7-1. Define reputation in the context of reputation risk.

7-2. Identify why reputation is a key asset to an organization.

7-3. Identify examples of external stakeholders.

7-4. Identify examples of organizational risks that can threaten reputation as a key asset.

7-5. Summarize the systemic approach to managing reputation risk.

7-6. Identify the three risk management principles that an organization must follow to implement risk management for risk to reputation.

Answers to Assignment 5 Questions

NOTE: These answers are provided to give students a basic understanding of acceptable types of responses. They often are not the only valid answers and are not intended to provide an exhaustive response to the questions.

Educational Objective 1

1-1. Intellectual property derives its value from the right of its owner to exclude others from using it.

1-2. Intellectual property owners historically have enforced their rights through civil suits.

1-3. The Paris Convention is significant to intellectual property rights because it was the first major international treaty designed to help people of one country obtain protection in other countries for their intellectual creations in the form of industrial property rights.

1-4. The intent of a trademark is to create a distinction of the products or services that the organization provides in the minds of its customers.

1-5. A trade secret is a practice, method, process, design, or other information used confidentially by an organization to maintain a competitive advantage.

Educational Objective 2

2-1. The three important features of copyright are creation, ownership, and duration.

2-2. These are the three criteria a work must meet to be considered copyrighted:

- The work must be original. It cannot be copied from another source.

- The work must be fixed in a tangible medium of expression that is permanently recorded. This could be in any manner of forms such as paper, video- or audiotape, or digital media.

- The work must have some degree of creativity. No set rule governs what constitutes enough creativity.

2-3. It is important to determine whether the organization or the employee owns the copyright because ownership of a copyright creates value for an organization. Therefore, copyright ownership must be determined to help establish the values exposed to loss and to ensure the organization owns what it believes it owns.

2-4. Examples of risk control measures that can be used for copyright loss exposures include notice, registration, restrictive covenants, responses to anticipated defenses, and licensing agreements.

2-5. Two benefits associated with registering a copyright are that registration provides reasonable, if not indisputable, evidence of ownership rights and that registration allows the copyright owner to collect statutory damages (up to $100,000 plus attorneys' fees) without having to prove actual monetary harm.

2-6. A restrictive covenant is any provision, clause, or agreement that, on termination of employment or contract, restricts the post-termination activities of the employee or contracting party.

Educational Objective 3

3-1. Trademarks are used by organizations to differentiate their products from their competitors'.

3-2. Three important features shared by trademarks, servicemarks, and trade dress are categories, creation, and duration.

3-3. The characteristic of an arbitrary mark that makes it memorable is its random nature.

3-4. A fanciful mark is a word or phrase that conjures up an image that is imaginative.

3-5. These are risk control measures that may be used for trademark and servicemark loss exposures:

- Notice

- Registration

- Searches and watches

- Licensing agreements

- Restrictive covenants

- Enforcement of rights

Educational Objective 4

4-1. The three types of patents are utility, design, and plant.

4-2. To be eligible for a patent in the United States, an invention must be new, useful, and nonobvious.

4-3. Many companies and inventors use monitoring firms to watch the newly published applications in order to protect their own patents or to object to a patent application.

4-4. These are the risk control measures that can be used for patent loss exposures:

- Notice

- Licensing agreements

- Restrictive covenants

- Freedom to operate search

4-5. The employment contract should define items of intellectual property (copyright, patent, or trade secret) that are covered by the agreement. The agreement should require full disclosure of any discoveries, inventions, improvements, or ideas, whether patentable or not, that the employee makes or conceives during work hours using materials, funds, or facilities supplied by the employer. The agreement should specify whether prior inventions are included in the agreement and should include confidentiality and nondisclosure language. The agreement may also include a provision in which the employee agrees not to use patents or trade secrets belonging to others in the course of the employee's employment. In the event of an infringement claim against the employer, this provision helps show that the employer was not willfully infringing.

Educational Objective 5

5-1. The most obvious loss exposure associated with trade secrets is that another entity might honestly recreate an organization's secret invention, process, or method and get it patented.

5-2. The starting point for the determination is whether the information regarding the invention, idea, or process has value and whether the information has really been treated as a secret.

5-3. These are the questions courts answer to determine trade secret status:

- How well is the secret known outside the business that owns the secret?

- How much of the secret is disclosed to employees of the business that owns the secret?

- What steps are taken to guard the secret?

- What is the secret's commercial value?

- How difficult would it be for someone else to acquire or duplicate the secret?

5-4. These are the risk control measures that can be used to ensure information confidentiality:

- Disclose the information only to those employees who need to know the information to perform their jobs

- Require a sign-in or similar security measure to gain access to the area where the secret information is used or maintained

- Control any documentation regarding the secret by using a safe, a "confidential" stamp, or a burn bag (a bag used to burn documents that are meant to be kept secret, in lieu of using a shredder)

- Require employees to sign a restrictive covenant in the form of a nondisclosure or a confidentiality agreement

Educational Objective 6

6-1. Methods organizations can use to safeguard some of their intellectual property include copyright, trademark, patent, and trade secret protection.

6-2. Protecting all of an organization's intellectual property is challenging because the essence of intellectual property is information and ideas.

6-3. When an organization is faced with unauthorized use of its intellectual property, it must quantify the resulting damage in order to recover. The property's monetary value is a necessary part of such quantification and any related litigation.

6-4. These are the most frequently used intellectual property valuation methodologies:

- The fair market value approach—assigns to a piece of intellectual property the value it would have on the open market were it to change hands between a willing buyer and a willing seller

- The income approach—assigns a current value to a piece of intellectual property based on the discounted cash flows the property would generate over its useful life

- The cost approach—assigns a value to a piece of intellectual property based on the amount the organization invested in its creation and development

Educational Objective 7

7-1. In the context of reputation risk, reputation is an intangible asset. It is a key determinant of future business prospects—resulting from a collection of perceptions and opinions, past and present—about an organization that resides in the consciousness of its stakeholders.

7-2. Reputation is a key asset to an organization because of its intrinsic, intangible value (its goodwill reserve or reputational equity) and because of its potential to generate (or erode) future value.

7-3. Examples of external stakeholders include shareholders, customers, suppliers, regulators, and governmental entities.

7-4. Examples of organizational risk that can threaten reputation as a key asset include legal and regulatory noncompliance, unethical behavior on the part of the board of directors or senior management, and the filing of major lawsuits.

7-5. In a systemic approach to managing reputation risk, the organization is considered within the context of a complex combination of available resources. Stakeholders have expectations regarding how these resources should be managed. The organization must work to gain the trust of stakeholders and assure them that resources are being integrated and optimized.

7-6. The three risk management principles that an organization must follow to implement risk management for risk to reputation are identify, evaluate, and prioritize reputational risks; develop and implement risk responses; and monitor and report.

Direct Your Learning

Legal and Regulatory Risk

Educational Objectives

After learning the content of this assignment, you should be able to:

1. Explain how civil law, criminal law, and regulation form the basis for legal and regulatory risk.

2. Describe the consequences of legal and regulatory risk to an organization.

3. Explain how each of the following is used to treat legal and regulatory risk:

   - Avoidance

   - Modification of an event's likelihood

   - Modification of an event's consequences

4. Describe the characteristics of these predominant legal systems:

   - Civil law (including Roman-French, German, and Scandinavian)

   - Common law

   - East Asian

   - Hindu

   - Islamic

   - Socialist-Communist

5. Distinguish between public international law and private international law.

6. Describe the legal foundations and the general scope of each of the following commercial liability loss exposures:

   - Premises and operations liability

   - Products and completed operations liability

6

- Automobile liability
- Workers compensation and employers liability

7. Given information on an organization's legal and regulatory risk exposures, assess the risk and recommend treatment options for modifying the likelihood and/or consequences.

Outline

Before starting a new assignment, briefly review the Educational Objectives of those preceding it.

For each assignment, you should define or describe each of the Key Words and Phrases and answer each of the Review and Application Questions.

Educational Objective 1
Explain how civil law, criminal law, and regulation form the basis for legal and regulatory risk.

Key Words and Phrases

Tort

Express contract

Implied contract

Valid contract

Void contract

Voidable contract

Unenforceable contract

Review Questions

1-1. Identify the categories of the major bases of legal and regulatory risk.

1-2. Distinguish between criminal law and civil law.

1-3. List the three categories of wrongful acts that constitute torts.

1-4. Explain how legal liability can arise from contracts.

1-5. Describe the requirements of agreement for an enforceable contract.

1-6. Explain how statutes modify the duties that organizations owe to others.

Application Question

1-7. Snowplow Operator clears one foot of snow from the parking lot of Office Building without being asked to do so. Snowplow Operator submits an invoice, which Office Building refuses to pay.

a. Describe the elements of an enforceable contract.

b. Explain which element of an enforceable contract is missing for Snowplow Operator.

Educational Objective 2
Describe the consequences of legal and regulatory risk to an organization.

Key Words and Phrases
Compensatory damages

Special damages

General damages

Punitive damages (exemplary damages)

Specific performance

Injunction

Review Questions

2-1. Identify the consequences of criminal acts.

2-2. Identify the two types of monetary damages that may be awarded in a civil suit.

2-3.   Explain why defense costs can be the most expensive loss for an organization.

2-4.   Describe the use of an injunction in a civil suit.

Educational Objective 3

Explain how each of the following is used to treat legal and regulatory risk:

- **Avoidance**
- **Modification of an event's likelihood**
- **Modification of an event's consequences**

Key Words and Phrases

Hazard

Privilege

Immunity

Comparative negligence

Last clear chance doctrine

Review Questions

3-1. Identify the ways to treat the negative aspects of legal and regulatory risk.

3-2. Describe the circumstances for which avoidance may be used as a risk treatment technique.

3-3. List the clauses that can be added to contracts to remove or limit liability.

3-4. Explain how unilateral notices can limit the likelihood of tort liability.

3-5. Explain how hazard control can be used to modify the likelihood of legal risk.

3-6. Describe the risk control areas a risk management professional should be concerned about for premises and operations risk exposures.

3-7. Describe the measures to reduce the likelihood of contractual liability.

3-8. Explain how a corporate code of conduct reduces the likelihood of statutory liability.

3-9. Identify the five defenses that are widely used in the litigation process.

3-10. Explain how participating in settlement negotiation can modify the consequences of tort liability.

3-11. Describe a defense used by organizations to modify the consequences of statutory liability.

Application Questions

3-12. Alderton Trampoline Company (Alderton) makes trampolines for residential use. What risk control measures might Alderton use for its products?

3-13. Waxton Road Building Contractor (Waxton) wants a bonus that rewards rapid completion included in its contract with the highway department. In addition to the bonus provision, explain how might the highway department further encourage Waxton to be on time?

Educational Objective 4

Describe the characteristics of these predominant legal systems:

- **Civil law (including Roman-French, German, and Scandinavian)**
- **Common law**
- **East Asian**
- **Hindu**
- **Islamic**
- **Socialist-Communist**

Review Questions

4-1.   Identify the two major legal systems.

4-2.   Name the three stages of a typical civil-law case.

4-3.   Describe the common-law legal system.

4-4. Explain why private-sector business legal principles, such as contracts and bankruptcy, are of little use within the socialist legal system.

Educational Objective 5
Distinguish between public international law and private international law.

Key Words and Phrases

Public international law

Private international law

Review Questions

5-1. Contrast public and private international law.

5-2. Define comity as it relates to private international law.

5-3. Explain the three areas of jurisdiction that courts in international cases must determine before presiding over a particular case.

Educational Objective 6

Describe the legal foundations and the general scope of each of the following commercial liability loss exposures:

- **Premises and operations liability**
- **Products and completed operations liability**
- **Automobile liability**
- **Workers compensation and employers liability**

Review Questions

6-1. The premises and operations liability exposure relates to liability for bodily injury or property damage caused by accidents arising from two sets of circumstances. Describe them.

6-2. Name the three elements a plaintiff must prove in order to recover in a products liability suit based on strict liability in tort.

6-3. Briefly describe common law and statutory law approaches to imposing auto liability solely on the basis of auto ownership.

6-4. Explain what a plaintiff must show to establish an auto owner's liability for negligent entrustment.

6-5. Explain how under an auto no-fault law, a verbal threshold differs from a monetary damages threshold.

6-6. Describe the situations in which an employer might be sued by an employee (or family members of an employee) for work-related injury.

Educational Objective 7

Given information on an organization's legal and regulatory risk exposures, assess the risk and recommend treatment options for modifying the likelihood and/or consequences.

Application Question

7-1. The risk manager for a chain of grocery stores is in the process of assessing the organization's legal and regulatory risks. As part of this process, risk treatment options must also be considered.

a. Describe the types of wrongful acts that constitute potential torts for this organization.

b. Explain how the risk manager could use modifying the likelihood of an event as a risk treatment method for torts.

Answers to Assignment 6 Questions

NOTE: These answers are provided to give students a basic understanding of acceptable types of responses. They often are not the only valid answers and are not intended to provide an exhaustive response to the questions.

Educational Objective 1

1-1. The major bases of legal and regulatory risk fall into these categories: torts, contracts, and statutes and regulations.

1-2. Criminal law is a classification of law that applies to acts that society deems so harmful to the public welfare that government is responsible for prosecuting and punishing the perpetrators. Civil law is a classification of law that applies to legal matters not governed by criminal law and that protects rights and provides remedies for breaches of duties owed to others. Civil law applies to all legal matters that are not crimes and involve private rights.

1-3. The three categories of wrongful acts that constitute torts are negligence, intentional torts, and strict liability torts.

1-4. Individuals and businesses can become liable based on the contract's terms or based on the terms that can be inferred from the contract, known as implied warranties.

1-5. The requirements for agreement include offer and acceptance. One party makes an offer that the other party accepts. Both parties must mutually understand and agree on the critical terms of the offer and the agreement.

1-6. Violating the duties imposed by a statute may be used as evidence that the organization breached the duty of care owed to another. Violating a statute also imposes legal liability on an organization regardless of whether the organization committed any tort or assumed any liability under a contract.

1-7. These answers apply to Snowplow Operator:

a. For a contract to be enforceable, four basic requirements must be met:

- Agreement (including offer and acceptance)—One party makes an offer that the other party accepts. Both parties must mutually understand and agree on the critical terms of the offer and the agreement.

- Consideration—Each party gives up something of value. Commonly, one party exchanges money for the other party's promise to perform some activity.

- Capacity to contract—The parties must have the legal ability to enter into contracts. A contracting party who is not of legal age, sane, or sober does not have the capacity to enter into a contract.

- Legal purpose—The contract must have a legal purpose and must not be opposed to public policy.

b. Snowplow Operator did not enter into an agreement with Office Building; therefore, no enforceable contract exists between Snowplow Operator and Office Building.

Educational Objective 2

2-1. The consequence of many criminal acts is incarceration for a specified period of time. Criminal acts can also result in monetary consequences, such as fines.

2-2. A wrongdoer in a civil suit will have to pay compensatory and noncompensatory monetary damages awarded by a court.

2-3. Defense costs can be expensive because many cases are so technical that they require the use of expert witnesses, whose fees can be significant. Even the cost of reproducing pertinent documents or obtaining witnesses can be significant. Beyond the substantial legal fees, the defendant is usually responsible for paying all costs imposed by the court, including jury fees, filing fees, and premiums on court bonds.

2-4. A court can use an injunction to order a party to refrain from engaging in a particular activity.

Educational Objective 3

3-1. The negative aspects of legal and regulatory risk can be treated through risk avoidance, modifying the likelihood of an event, and modifying the consequences of an event.

3-2. Avoidance is usually used as a risk treatment technique only in high probability-high severity situations.

3-3. The clauses that can be added to contracts to remove or limit liability are waivers, hold-harmless agreements, exculpatory agreements, and unilateral notices.

3-4. Unilateral notices can limit liability if the notices are posted so that they are physically apparent, expressed in language the other party understands (which is a concern if the other party does not speak the language used), and reasonable in extent (not forever or applicable to every possible risk).

3-5. Hazard control involves implementing risk control measures that eliminate or reduce hazards.

3-6. For premises and operations, these are the risk control areas of particular concern to a risk management professional:

- Parking lots
- Building entrances and exits
- Walking surfaces
- Merchandise displays and counters
- Escalators, elevators, and stairways

3-7. Measures to reduce the likelihood for contractual liability include having most if not all contracts reviewed by counsel, preferably before they are signed, and using written contracts rather than oral contracts that rely on memory and word of mouth. This is true even in long-term business relationships. Care must also be taken when committing an agreement to writing that the contract accurately reflects the intentions of both parties.

3-8. A corporate code of conduct provides all employees with the organization's mission and commitment to ethical behavior and outlines applicable policies and the importance of regulatory compliance. In global organizations, the code of conduct must reflect the various legal and regulatory environments of all of the jurisdictions in which the organization conducts business.

3-9. The five defenses are:

- Legal privilege

- Immunity

- Comparative negligence

- Last clear chance doctrine

- Assumption of risk

3-10. An organization's risk management professional (and perhaps, for major claims, its senior management) should take an active interest in lawsuit negotiations. Before a final verdict, settlement negotiations might offer opportunities to resolve the suit more favorably than would the court.

3-11. A defense commonly pled by organizations in statutory cases is that the statute was unconstitutional or was too vague or ambiguous to be enforceable. If the statute has already been tested on this defense and upheld by a higher court, it will likely not be effective.

3-12. Alderton should consider the following risk control measures in manufacturing its products:

- Design trampolines with safety in mind, especially considering that most users may be children

- Test the trampolines before, during, and after production

- Adhere to established production and quality controls

- Be clear and accurate in any instructions for use

- Provide manuals for assembly and use of trampolines

3-13. To encourage Waxton's on-time completion, the highway department may consider including a liquidated damages provision in the contract. Such a provision would penalize Waxton in the event of delayed completion.

Educational Objective 4

4-1. The two major legal systems in the majority of countries are the civil-law system and the common-law system.

4-2. The three stages of a typical civil-law case are these:

- The preliminary stage

- The evidence stage

- The decision stage

4-3. In the common-law legal system, a judge interprets the facts of a case, examines precedents, and makes a decision based on the facts in the current case.

4-4. Private-sector business legal principles, such as contracts, commercial law, torts, property, and bankruptcy, are of little use within a socialist system. Public law replaces private-sector legal principles. For example, because the government owns all property and production, all contract law is public. In a socialist country, the socialist political party controls and influences the entire legal system, including the courts. All decisions from the courts, although independent in nature, are subject to party control or revision.

Educational Objective 5

5-1. Public international law concerns the interrelation of nation states and is governed by treaties and other international agreements, while private international law involves disputes between individuals or corporations in different countries.

5-2. Comity is the practice by which one country recognizes, within its own territory or in its courts, another country's institutions.

5-3. Courts in international cases must determine whether they have jurisdiction over the person or entity (*in personam* jurisdiction) and over the subject matter (*in res* jurisdiction) and if they have jurisdiction to render the particular judgment in the case.

Educational Objective 6

6-1. The premises and operations liability loss exposure relates to liability arising from bodily injury or property damage caused either by an accident that occurs on an organization's owned, leased, or rented premises or by an accident that arises out of the organization's ongoing (as opposed to completed) operations but occurs away from the premises.

6-2. To recover in a products liability suit based on strict liability, the plaintiff must prove three elements:

- The product was defective when it left the manufacturer's or supplier's custody or control.

- The defective condition made the product unreasonably dangerous.

- The defective product was the proximate cause of the plaintiff's injury.

6-3. Under the common law, ownership of an auto does not in itself make the owner liable for injury or damage caused by someone else's negligent operation of the vehicle. Several states have passed laws making an auto owner liable for damages arising from any person's operation of the auto with the owner's express or implied permission.

6-4. To establish liability for negligent entrustment, the plaintiff must show that the party entrusting the vehicle knew or should have known of the driver's incompetence, inexperience, or reckless tendencies.

6-5. A verbal threshold defines the seriousness of injuries beyond which the right to sue is allowed. A monetary damages threshold sets a dollar limit that, if exceeded, allows an auto accident victim to sue.

6-6. An employer might be sued by an employee or family member if (1) injury to the employee was intentional, (2) the employee's injury caused by the employer's negligence or other torts resulted in a loss of consortium for the employee's spouse, or (3) the injury resulted from the employer's negligence while acting in some capacity other than an employer.

Educational Objective 7

7-1. These answers apply to the grocery store operation:

a. Wrongful acts fall into three categories: negligence, intentional torts, and strict liability torts. Negligence is an unintentional tort in which individuals, such as customers, may be exposed to unreasonable danger when the owner of a premises fails to exercise the duty of care required by law. For example, if a spill occurs in one of the grocery store aisles and is not cleaned up promptly, a customer could be injured by slipping and falling. Intentional torts are acts that are intended by the tortfeasor; however, the consequences are not intended. For the grocery store operation, such intentional torts might include charges of false imprisonment by an alleged shoplifter detained by the store's security force. False advertising or intimidating competitors is another potential intentional tort. Strict liability torts arise when an organization engages in a hazardous activity or in certain products liability cases. Based on the grocery stores' operations, it is unlikely the organization would be involved in strict liability torts.

b. Modifying the likelihood of an event arising from legal risk is often called loss prevention. The risk manager could prevent or reduce the likelihood of litigation by removing or limiting the organization's legal obligations to others by adding clauses to contracts to remove or limit liability. For example, the organization could contract with an outside firm to handle security issues and include a hold-harmless agreement in the contract. Hazard control is another method used to modify the likelihood of legal risk; it involves implementing risk control measures to eliminate or reduce hazards. The organization could institute a policy for handling spills on the premises that would require prompt cleanup, closing off aisles, or putting up signs warning of the dangerous conditions where the spill occurred. Proper maintenance and housekeeping can also reduce the chance of injury and prevent accidents from happening.

Direct Your Learning

Management Liability

Educational Objectives

After learning the content of this assignment, you should be able to:

1. Describe the liability loss exposures of a corporation's directors and officers, with specific reference to their responsibilities and duties and the types of suits that may be made against them.

2. Describe the major types of claims associated with employment practices liability (EPL) loss exposures.

3. Describe the legal foundations for fiduciary liability loss exposures, with specific reference to the Employee Retirement Income Security Act (ERISA) and the duties of employee benefit plan fiduciaries.

Outline

▶ **Directors and Officers Liability Loss Exposures**
   A. Corporations and the Role of Directors and Officers
   B. Major Responsibilities and Duties of Directors and Officers
      1. Duty of Care
      2. Duty of Loyalty
      3. Duty of Disclosure
      4. Duty of Obedience
   C. Types of Suits Made Against Directors and Officers
      1. Derivative Suits
      2. Nonderivative Suits
      3. Class Actions
   D. Indemnification of Directors and Officers
   E. Controlling D&O Liability Loss Exposures
▶ **Employment Practices Liability Loss Exposures**
   A. Discrimination Claims
   B. Wrongful Termination Claims
   C. Sexual Harassment Claims
   D. Retaliation Claims
   E. Other Types of EPL Claims
▶ **Fiduciary Liability Loss Exposures**
   A. ERISA
   B. Duties and Liabilities of Employee Benefit Plan Fiduciaries
      1. Specific Duties
      2. Standards and Liability
   C. HIPAA

Perform a final review before your exam, but don't cram. Give yourself between two and four hours to go over the course work.

▶▶

For each assignment, you should define or describe each of the Key Words and Phrases and answer each of the Review and Application Questions.

Educational Objective 1

Describe the liability loss exposures of a corporation's directors and officers, with specific reference to their responsibilities and duties and the types of suits that may be made against them.

Key Words and Phrases

Fiduciary duty

Business judgment rule

Ultra vires

Review Questions

1-1. Describe the major functions of a corporation's board of directors.

1-2. Describe the four fiduciary duties of the directors and officers of a corporation.

1-3. Compare derivative and nonderivative suits.

1-4. Describe a typical basis for class action lawsuits against directors and officers of a corporation, and provide an example of a common allegation.

1-5. Discuss why corporations might settle claims against their directors and officers even if they believe they have defenses to the claims.

1-6. Discuss how settlement of claims against a corporation's directors and officers can present problems for indemnification of the directors and officers.

1-7. Discuss the reasons that risk control should be a central part of the management of directors and officers (D&O) loss exposures.

Educational Objective 2
Describe the major types of claims associated with employment practices liability (EPL) loss exposures.

Review Questions

2-1. Name the four major types of employment practices liability (EPL) claims.

2-2. Describe the role of the Equal Employment Opportunity Commission (EEOC) in workplace discrimination claims.

2-3. Explain how the legal doctrine of "employment at will" affects the employment relationship between employers and employees.

2-4. Describe the exceptions to "employment at will" that may make it more difficult to discharge (fire) employees without adverse consequences.

2-5. Name the types of EPL offenses in which the law recognize claims of a hostile work environment.

Educational Objective 3

Describe the legal foundations for fiduciary liability loss exposures, with specific reference to the Employee Retirement Income Security Act (ERISA) and the duties of employee benefit plan fiduciaries.

Review Questions

3-1. Describe the basic type of claim that constitutes fiduciary liability loss exposures.

3-2. Name the federal law that governs all types and sizes of employee benefit plans.

3-3. Explain who qualifies as an employee benefit plan fiduciary under ERISA.

3-4. Summarize the fiduciary duties of an employee benefit plan fiduciary.

3-5. Name who, besides the fiduciary, can be held liable for breaches of fiduciary duty committed by a fiduciary who is also an employee or agent of the employer sponsoring the employee benefit plans.

Application Question

3-6. Serge is the HR generalist at Greenly Cable Company (GCC). He recently hired several new customer service representatives to accommodate an increase in services that GCC offers. This growth in the number of employees makes GCC subject to HIPAA (Health Insurance Portability and Accountability Act of 1996).

   a. Describe the four major objectives that HIPAA accomplishes.

b. What would be a particular concern from an insurance point of view for employers subject to HIPAA?

Answers to Assignment 7 Questions

NOTE: These answers are provided to give students a basic understanding of acceptable types of responses. They often are not the only valid answers and are not intended to provide an exhaustive response to the questions.

Educational Objective 1

1-1. The board of directors establishes corporate policy, makes major business and financial decisions, and appoints the corporation's executive officers to manage the corporation's daily operations.

1-2. The first fiduciary duty is the duty of care. Directors and officers must discharge their duties with the care that a person in a similar position would reasonably believe appropriate under similar circumstances. The second fiduciary duty is the duty of loyalty. Directors and officers must discharge their duties in a manner the director reasonably believes to be in the best interest of the corporation; they may not own or operate businesses that compete with the corporation. The third fiduciary duty is the duty of disclosure. Directors and officers must disclose material facts to all persons who have a right to know such facts and would not otherwise be able to obtain them. The fourth fiduciary duty is the duty of obedience (to the law). Directors and officers must perform their duties according to applicable statutes and the terms of the corporate charter.

1-3. A derivative suit is a lawsuit brought by one or more shareholders in the name of the corporation. Any damages recovered go directly to the corporation, not to the plaintiff-stockholder(s). Nonderivative suits against directors and officers are not made in the name of the corporation and may be initiated by customers, competitors, employees, creditors, governmental entities, or other persons outside the corporation.

1-4. Many class actions against directors and officers are based on wrongful acts related to securities. A typical securities class action lawsuit commonly makes one or more of these allegations: the corporation's public statements contained material misrepresentations or omissions, alleged misrepresentations or omissions artificially inflated the corporation's stock price, or insiders profitably sold their personal holdings in the corporation's stock while the stock price was artificially inflated.

1-5. Defense costs and the amount of time required to prepare an adequate defense can be devastating. Therefore, corporations in many situations make payment to settle claims against their directors and officers.

1-6. Often, indemnification of directors and officers under common law requires that the corporate officers and directors successfully defend against a suit. When a suit is settled, it is terminated with no determination of wrongdoing. Therefore, it is not clear whether the directors and officers are entitled to indemnification.

1-7. Claims against corporate directors and officers can create significant defense and settlement costs. Key executives must devote significant amounts of their time defending against claims and the potential loss of reputation for the corporation. Although D&O liability insurance can transfer some of the financial risk of these suits, it cannot restore a corporation's reputation. Loss of a corporation's reputation can damage customer relationships, hinder access to the capital markets, and make it difficult to attract highly qualified executives. Therefore, risk control should be a central part of the management of D&O loss exposures.

▶▶

Educational Objective 2

2-1. Four major types of EPL claims are these:

- Discrimination claims

- Wrongful termination claims

- Sexual harassment claims

- Retaliation claims

2-2. After an employee files charges of workplace discrimination, the EEOC notifies the employer of the claim and investigates whether there is reasonable cause to believe discrimination occurred. The employer may opt to resolve a charge through mediation or settlement. Employees do not have to submit a complaint to the EEOC to sue their employers, and dismissal of a complaint by the EEOC is not a bar to a suit by the employee.

2-3. Employment at will allows employers or employees to terminate the employment relationship with or without cause at any time.

2-4. Several states base an exception to employment at will on the theory of implied contract. Under this theory, an implied contract of employment is formed if the employer makes oral or written representations to employees regarding job security or disciplinary procedures. The implied contract can prevent the employer from firing an employee without cause. Another exception, applied by courts in a minority of states, is that employment at will is subject to a covenant of good faith, thus requiring just cause for firing an employee.

2-5. The law recognizes claims of hostile work environment in the contexts of sexual harassment, discrimination because of race, and discrimination because of disability.

Educational Objective 3

3-1. The basic type of claim that constitutes fiduciary liability loss exposures is a claim made by the beneficiaries of an employee benefit plan against the plan officials (or fiduciaries) for breach of their fiduciary duties.

3-2. The Employee Retirement Income Security Act (ERISA) is the federal law that governs all types and sizes of employee benefit plans.

3-3. Practically anyone whose role in employee benefits involves discretionary control or judgment in the design, administration, funding, or management of a benefit plan or in the management of its assets is a fiduciary under ERISA.

3-4. The fiduciary duties of an employee benefit plan fiduciary can be summarized as follows:

- Loyalty: A fiduciary's actions must be in the best interests of the plan and all of its participants and beneficiaries.

- Prudence: A fiduciary must perform his or her duties with the care, skill, prudence, and diligence of a prudent person familiar with such matters.

- Diversification: A fiduciary must ensure that the plan's investments are sufficiently diversified to minimize the risk of large losses.

- Adherence: A fiduciary must act according to the plan documents and applicable law.

3-5. The employer may be held vicariously liable for breaches of fiduciary duty committed by its employees or agents.

3-6. These answers pertain to Greenly Cable Company.

a. These are the four major objectives that HIPAA accomplishes:

- Sets standards for health insurance "portability" by providing credit against preexisting condition exclusion periods for prior health coverage

- Limits exclusions for preexisting medical conditions

- Prohibits discrimination in enrollment and in premiums charged to employees and their dependents based on health-related factors

- Improves disclosure about group health plans

b. Of particular concern from an insurance point of view is that HIPAA calls for the protection of employee medical information and subjects the employer and fiduciaries to penalties for failure to comply.

Direct Your Learning

Human Resource Risk

Educational Objectives

After learning the content of this assignment, you should be able to:

1. Describe the human resource potential of an organization and the factors that affect it.

2. Describe the following personnel causes of loss:
   - Work-related injury and illness
   - Retirement and resignation
   - Work-related violence

3. Explain how the following methods help risk managers assess personnel loss exposures:
   - Risk assessment questionnaires
   - Loss histories
   - Other records and documents
   - Flowcharts and organizational charts
   - Personal inspections
   - Expertise within and beyond the organization

4. Explain how the following risk control techniques can be used to mitigate losses arising from work-related injury and illness:
   - Avoidance
   - Loss prevention
   - Loss reduction
   - Separation and duplication

8

Educational Objectives, continued

5. Explain how to mitigate losses arising from work-related violence.

6. Given information on an organization's human resource risk exposures, assess the risk and recommend treatment options.

Outline

▶ **Human Resource Potential**
  A. Health and Education of the General Population
  B. Proper Personnel Selection Procedures
  C. Preservation of Employees' Existing Productive Capabilities
  D. Rehabilitation of Injured or Ill Employees
  E. Retention of Productive Employees

▶ **Types of Personnel Losses**
  A. Work-Related Injury and Illness
    1. Injury Causes of Loss
    2. Illness Causes of Loss
  B. Retirement and Resignation
  C. Work-Related Violence
    1. Workplace Violence
    2. Kidnap and Ransom

▶ **Assessing Personnel Loss Exposures**
  A. Risk Assessment Questionnaires
  B. Loss Histories
  C. Other Records and Documents
  D. Flowcharts and Organizational Charts
  E. Personal Inspections
  F. Expertise Within and Beyond the Organization

▶ **Risk Treatment for Work-Related Injury and Illness**
  A. Avoidance
  B. Loss Prevention
    1. Safety Engineering
    2. Workplace Design
  C. Loss Reduction
  D. Separation and Duplication

▶ **Risk Treatment for Work-Related Violence**
  A. Workplace Violence
  B. Kidnap and Ransom

▶ **Assessing and Treating Human Resource Risk**
  A. Case Facts
  B. Case Analysis Tools
  C. Overview of Steps
  D. Identify and Analyze Hightower's Human Resource Risk Exposures
  E. Recommend Risk Treatment Options

When reviewing for your exam, remember to allot time for frequent breaks.

For each assignment, you should define or describe each of the Key Words and Phrases and answer each of the Review and Application Questions.

Educational Objective 1

Describe the human resource potential of an organization and the factors that affect it.

Review Questions

1-1. Identify the factors that affect an organization's human resource potential.

1-2. Explain the correlation between a population's physical and mental health and its human resource potential.

1-3. Identify the organizational activities associated with preservation of employees' existing productive capabilities.

▶▶

1-4.   Describe the goal of rehabilitation of injured or ill employees.

Application Question

1-5.   A large percentage of the most productive inside sales representatives for Gamma, a financial services firm, have either left or are considering leaving to work for a local competitor. Concerned about the loss of valuable personnel, the risk management professional for the organization investigates the cause of the resignations. She determines the reason is not for a substantially higher salary. Instead, the answers she hears include a safer and less stressful work environment and promised opportunities for promotion. The most common response she gets, however, is that the most respected and productive co-workers have already left. The new firm also has a reputation of providing scholarships to promising students in the local community in financial need. Identify the human resource factors that could be influencing the competing firm's appeal.

Educational Objective 2

Describe the following personnel causes of loss:

- **Work-related injury and illness**
- **Retirement and resignation**
- **Work-related violence**

Review Questions

2-1. Identify the difference between an injury and an illness.

2-2. Explain why the distinction between injury and illness is relevant in workplace settings.

2-3. Identify the general categories into which the majority of work-related injury causes of loss in manufacturing and retail businesses fall.

2-4.   Identify the worksite causes of loss likely to produce disabling illnesses.

2-5.   Identify what determines the extent of productivity loss when an employee
       retires or resigns.

2-6.   Identify the two primary types of work-related violence.

Educational Objective 3

Explain how the following methods help risk managers assess personnel loss exposures:

- **Risk assessment questionnaires**
- **Loss histories**
- **Other records and documents**
- **Flowcharts and organizational charts**
- **Personal inspections**
- **Expertise within and beyond the organization**

Review Questions

3-1. Describe the strength and weakness of using risk assessment questionnaires in identifying personnel loss exposures.

3-2. Identify the types of information provided to the risk management professional by reviewing an organization's loss history.

3-3. Identify two insurance industry sources of information that are useful to a risk management professional in assessing an organization's potential personnel losses resulting from death or disability.

Educational Objective 4

Explain how the following risk control techniques can be used to mitigate losses arising from work-related injury and illness:

- **Avoidance**
- **Loss prevention**
- **Loss reduction**
- **Separation and duplication**

Key Words and Phrases

Ergonomics

Human factors engineering

Biomechanics

Review Questions

4-1. Identify the four categories of risk control techniques that may be applied to work-related injury and illness.

4-2. Identify examples of loss prevention techniques associated with physical causes of loss.

4-3. Identify examples of loss prevention techniques associated with procedural causes of loss.

4-4. Identify the physical activities associated with manual materials handling.

4-5. Identify examples of physical injuries that may result from improperly laid out workstations.

4-6. Describe the concept of biomechanics.

4-7. Summarize the rehabilitation process.

4-8. Contrast separation and duplication.

Educational Objective 5
Explain how to mitigate losses arising from work-related violence.

Review Questions

5-1. Identify the five key areas in which risk control measures can be used for workplace violence from co-workers.

5-2. Identify risk control measures that can be used to address risk associated with the termination process.

5-3.   Identify the most effective way to control a kidnap and ransom loss.

5-4.   Identify the advantages of a kidnap, ransom, and extortion insurance policy.

Application Question

5-5.   An organization is opening a manufacturing plant in a foreign country considered a high-risk area. Identify measures the organization's risk manager should implement to reduce the possibility of a kidnap and ransom situation.

Educational Objective 6

Given information on an organization's human resource risk exposures, assess the risk and recommend treatment options.

Application Question

6-1. A large percentage of the most productive inside sales representatives for Gamma, a financial services firm, have either left or are considering leaving to work for a local competitor. Concerned about the loss of valuable personnel, Gamma's risk management professional investigates the cause of the resignations. She determines that Gamma's workers are not leaving to pursue a substantially higher salary. Instead, she discovers that the local competitor offers a safer and less stressful work environment and opportunities for promotion. The competitor also provides scholarships to promising local students in financial need, a practice that has elevated its prestige in the community.

   a.   Explain the human resource factors that apply to this case.

   b.   Gamma asks its risk management professional to help it establish a succession plan for when a senior partner retires. What should the risk management professional suggest?

Answers to Assignment 8 Questions

NOTE: These answers are provided to give students a basic understanding of acceptable types of responses. They often are not the only valid answers and are not intended to provide an exhaustive response to the questions.

Educational Objective 1

1-1. These are the factors that affect an organization's human resource potential:

- Health and education of the general population

- Proper personnel selection procedures

- Preservation of employees' existing productive capabilities

- Rehabilitation of injured or ill employees

- Retention of productive employees

1-2. If a population enjoys good physical and mental health, tends to live a long time, and is well educated, an organization is more likely to be able to select employees with promising human resource potential than if the population as a whole does not have those positive characteristics.

1-3. Organizational activities associated with preservation of employees' existing productive capabilities include preventing or reducing disabling injuries and illnesses on or off the job, dissatisfaction with the job, and work-related violence.

1-4. The goal of rehabilitation of injured or ill employees is to speed their recovery, restoring as fully as possible their pre-injury or illness physical, intellectual, social, and interpersonal skills.

1-5. These are the human resource factors that could be influencing the competing firm's appeal:

- The competing firm has demonstrated its support of the local general population's education by providing scholarships.

- The fact that the most respected and productive co-workers have already been hired by the new firm is an indication it is using sound personnel selection, which in turn has encouraged other former co-workers to join the new firm.

- Providing a safer and less stressful working environment preserves the employees' existing productive capacities.

Educational Objective 2

2-1. An injury is usually caused by an external physical force exerting stress on the human body, resulting in some externally manifested damage such as a laceration, a fracture, a contusion, or an amputation. By contrast, an illness usually develops more slowly as the result of some organic or inorganic agent being absorbed, ingested, inhaled, or injected that impairs a function of a body.

2-2. In workplace settings, the distinction between injury and illness is relevant because the types of risk controls often applied to reducing the frequency or severity of particular disabilities depend on whether those disabilities arise from sudden external events (considered injuries) or from prolonged exposure to harmful conditions or a sudden harmful condition that does not immediately manifest itself (considered illnesses).

2-3. The general categories into which the majority of work-related injury causes of loss in manufacturing and retail businesses fall are machinery and equipment use, materials handling, vehicle fleet operations, and physical conditions of premises.

2-4. Worksite causes of loss likely to produce disabling illnesses are long-term chemical exposures, noise levels, ergonomic stress, radiation, temperature extremes, and poor air quality.

2-5. When an employee retires or resigns, the extent of the productivity loss depends on how quickly the employee can be replaced.

2-6. The two primary types of work-related violence are workplace violence and kidnap and ransom.

Educational Objective 3

3-1. The strength of using risk assessment questionnaires is that the questions are universally relevant in identifying an organization's personnel loss exposures. The weakness is that they cannot uncover all loss exposures characteristic to a specific industry or organization.

3-2. An organization's loss histories might provide these types of information:

- Mortality and disability rates

- Retirement trends

- Voluntary and involuntary employee separation histories

3-3. Two insurance industry sources of information that are useful to a risk management professional in assessing an organization's potential personnel losses are these:

- Mortality tables, which provide information regarding death rates. Assuming no adverse selection, the larger the organization, the closer its mortality rates will be to the applicable mortality table.

- Morbidity tables, which provide information regarding the frequency of illness.

Educational Objective 4

4-1. The four categories of risk control techniques that may be applied to work-related injury and illness are avoidance, loss prevention, loss reduction, and separation and duplication.

4-2.   Examples of loss prevention techniques associated with physical causes of loss include these:

- Materials substitution
- Isolation
- Wet methods
- Guarding
- Ventilation
- Maintenance
- Housekeeping
- Personal protective equipment (PPE)

4-3.   Examples of loss prevention techniques associated with procedural causes of loss include these:

- Process change
- Education and training
- Standard operating procedures
- Proper supervision
- Medical controls
- Job rotation

4-4.   The physical activities associated with manual materials handling include lifting, pulling, dragging, pushing, and transferring objects or materials.

4-5.   Examples of physical injuries that may result from improperly laid out workstations include vision difficulties, spinal strain, and poor posture.

4-6.   Biomechanics views people as a system of skeletal levers and muscular motors that exert force to achieve given results.

4-7.   Rehabilitation is the process of restoring an injured and disabled person to his or her highest attainable level of functioning and independence in self-care, vocational, and recreational activities.

4-8.   Separation of loss exposures involves arranging an organization's activities and resources so that no single event can cause simultaneous losses to all of them. Duplication involves creating backup facilities or assets to be used only if the primary activity or asset suffers a loss.

Educational Objective 5

5-1. These are the five key areas in which risk control measures can be used for workplace violence from co-workers:

- Hiring process

- Supervisor training

- Written policies

- Procedural safeguards

- Termination process

5-2. Risk control measures that can be used to address risk associated with the termination process involve establishing and following termination procedures, which include a termination meeting, a termination letter/package, an escort from the building, and other security precautions such as return of keys and identification badges.

5-3. The most effective way to control a kidnap and ransom loss is to prevent it.

5-4. The advantages of a kidnap, ransom, and extortion insurance policy include that it provides access to experts who can advise company officials during a kidnapping and who will negotiate with the kidnappers on the company's behalf. Kidnap, ransom, and extortion insurance also covers the evacuation, medical, and rehabilitation expenses of insured employees.

5-5. Measures the organization's risk manager should implement to reduce the possibility of a kidnap and ransom situation include maintaining a low profile. For example, company logos or other indications of company ownership can be removed from vehicles, clothing, and equipment. Company functions such as meetings and social events should, if possible, not be advertised outside the group of individuals who will attend. Wearing expensive jewelry and clothes or driving expensive vehicles should be discouraged. Aside from maintaining a low profile, an organization can implement additional measures such as employing bodyguards, housing employees in walled or secured compounds, using armored vehicles for transport, and providing bulletproof vests or body armor for employees to wear.

Educational Objective 6

6-1. These answers apply to the Gamma case:

a. The competing firm has demonstrated its support of the local population's education by providing scholarships. That may positively influence the quality and potential productivity of the firm's future employees, but it is not likely a direct motivating factor for an employee of another firm to leave his or her job and work there. That the most respected and productive Gamma workers have already been hired by the new firm indicates that the new firm is using sound personnel selection. Providing a safer and less stressful working environment preserves the employees' existing productive capacities. The differences between the firms combined with the new firm's promised opportunities for promotion have affected Gamma's ability to retain its employees.

b. The first step of identifying the key person is not an issue in this case—it is the senior partner. Recognizing that the senior partner's retirement is not preventable in the long run, the risk management professional should focus the succession plan on reducing the severity of the financial consequences when retirement does occur. The plan should determine which other people within Gamma can fill in for the key person, either temporarily or permanently. These individuals should be trained ahead of time. Another risk control technique is to spread key functions among a number of different employees so that when the senior partner retires, others can quickly fill in.

C

Direct Your Learning

Environmental Risk

Educational Objectives

After learning the content of this assignment, you should be able to:

1. Explain how an organization can incur environmental liability under tort, contract, or statutory law.

2. Describe the environmental loss exposures that might cause property, personnel, and net income losses.

3. Summarize the basic purpose and distinguishing features of each of the environmental statutes described.

4. Describe the following aspects of environmental risk management:

   • The process for identifying environmental loss exposures

   • The unique characteristics of environmental loss exposures

   • How to overcome difficulties in managing environmental loss exposures

5. Describe the factors and process for environmental risk assessment.

6. Describe environmental risk control measures, the hierarchy in which they should be used, and the considerations involved in their selection.

7. Explain how climate change can increase risk for organizations.

8. Given information on an organization's environmental risk exposures, assess the risk and recommend treatment options.

Outline

▶ **Legal Foundations for Environmental Liability**
  A. Tort Liability
     1. Negligence
     2. Intentional Torts
     3. Strict Liability
  B. Contractual Liability
  C. Environmental Statutes
  D. Enforcement of Environmental Laws
▶ **Other Environmental Loss Exposures**
  A. Property Loss Exposures
  B. Personnel Loss Exposures
  C. Net Income Loss Exposures
▶ **Environmental Statutes**
  A. Clean Water Act
  B. Clean Air Act
  C. Motor Carrier Act
  D. Toxic Substance Control Act
  E. Resource Conservation and Recovery Act
  F. Comprehensive Environmental Response, Compensation, and Liability Act
  G. Oil Pollution Act
▶ **Environmental Risk Management**
  A. Identifying Environmental Loss Exposures
  B. Unique Characteristics of Environmental Loss Exposures
  C. Overcoming Difficulties in Managing Environmental Loss Exposures
▶ **Environmental Risk Assessment**
  A. Environmental Risk Assessment Factors
  B. Environmental Risk Assessment Process
     1. Create an Assessment Plan
     2. Assemble the Team
     3. Gather Information to Identify Loss Exposures
     4. Analyze Environmental Loss Exposures

▶ **Environmental Risk Control**
  A. Source Reduction
  B. Source Treatment
     1. Recovery Processes
     2. Physical and Chemical Treatment Processes
     3. Thermal Processes
     4. Biological Processes
  C. Disposal
  D. Risk Control Measure Hierarchy
  E. Risk Control Measure Selection Considerations
▶ **Climate Change Risk**
  A. Climate Change Debate
  B. Types of Climate Change Risks
  C. Climate Change Risk Treatment
     1. Risk Control
     2. Risk Finance
     3. Risk Transfer
▶ **Assessing and Treating Environmental Risk**
  A. Case Facts
  B. Case Analysis Tools
  C. Overview of Steps
  D. Environmental Risk Assessment
  E. Treatment Options

Repetition helps students learn. Read, write, and repeat key points for each assignment.

For each assignment, you should define or describe each of the Key Words and Phrases and answer each of the Review and Application Questions.

Educational Objective 1

Explain how an organization can incur environmental liability under tort, contract, or statutory law.

Review Questions

1-1. Give an example of pollution liability based on each of these:

a. Negligence

b. Intentional tort

c. Strict liability

1-2. Explain how some environmental statutes create strict liability for polluters.

1-3. Decide what, in addition to a review of an organization's physical facilities, an Environmental Protection Agency (EPA) evaluation of compliance considers.

Application Question

1-4. For each of the pollution incidents described, identify the legal grounds that might be used to impose liability on the polluter:

    a. A kitchen remodeler used contact cement to affix counter tops in a family's kitchen. The family's young children were sickened by fumes from the contact cement.

    b. A crematorium's emissions strictly met all standards imposed by relevant statutes and ordinances. However, a public school district sought an injunction against the crematorium for certain hours of the day on the basis that the crematorium's emissions prevented the students of a nearby school from being able to enjoy their daily recess periods.

c. An auto body shop disposed of old paint and solvents for several years by dumping them in the woods of a neglected public park that was adjacent to the body shop's premises. The body shop's toxic waste disposal methods were discovered by a civic group that dedicated itself to reclaiming the park.

Educational Objective 2
Describe the environmental loss exposures that might cause property, personnel, and net income losses.

Review Questions

2-1. Explain how an organization might incur property losses as a result of environmental pollution.

2-2. Explain how environmental pollution might result in personnel losses.

2-3. Explain how net income losses might arise as a result of environmental pollution.

Educational Objective 3
Summarize the basic purpose and distinguishing features of each of the environmental statutes described.

Review Questions

3-1. Summarize the purpose of each of the following environmental statutes:

　　a. Clean Water Act

　　b. Clean Air Act

　　c. Motor Carrier Act of 1980

    d. Toxic Substance Control Act

3-2. Describe the purpose of the financial responsibility requirements for permit holders under the Resource Conservation and Recovery Act (RCRA).

3-3. Describe the purpose of the Comprehensive Environmental Response, Compensation, and Liability Act (CERCLA).

3-4. Describe the financial responsibility requirements under the Oil Pollution Act (OPA).

Educational Objective 4

Describe the following aspects of environmental risk management:

- **The process for identifying environmental loss exposures**
- **The unique characteristics of environmental loss exposures**
- **How to overcome difficulties in managing environmental loss exposures**

Review Questions

4-1. Summarize the three-step process that can be used to identify environmental loss exposures in developing an environmental risk management strategy.

4-2. Describe five of the unique characteristics of environmental loss exposures that must be considered when developing a plan to manage them.

4-3. Explain why environmental loss exposures are often difficult to identify.

4-4. Explain how advances in technology can change environmental loss exposures.

4-5. Describe the internal and external resources that can help overcome the difficulty of identifying environmental loss exposures.

Educational Objective 5
Describe the factors and process for environmental risk assessment.

Key Words and Phrases
Population at risk

Materials accounting

Compliance audit

Review Questions

5-1.   Identify ways in which an organization might use environmental risk assessments.

5-2.   Distinguish between environmental risk assessments that are quantitative and those that are qualitative.

5-3.   Identify the characteristics of a population at risk that a risk management professional should consider when evaluating existing or potential areas of contamination.

5-4.   List the four steps in the environmental risk assessment process.

Application Question

5-5. Amalgamated Paint Company plans to expand operations of one of its subsidiaries to include production of a solvent that is highly toxic if inhaled or ingested. Describe the appropriate risk assessment factors Amalgamated's risk manager should consider when assessing this loss exposure.

Educational Objective 6
Describe environmental risk control measures, the hierarchy in which they should be used, and the considerations involved in their selection.

Key Words and Phrases

Source reduction

Source treatment

Solidification, stabilization, and encapsulation processes

Review Questions

6-1. Identify basic risk control measures for source reduction.

6-2. Describe how these source treatment methods modify pollutants that have already been produced:

a. Recovery processes

b. Physical and chemical treatment processes

c. Thermal processes

    d. Biological processes

6-3. Identify considerations that can influence selection of risk control measures to manage environmental loss exposures.

Application Question

6-4. Amalgamated Paint Company's (APC's) previous management purchased 200 acres of land near the company's largest production facility as a disposal site for toxic waste, which is a byproduct of APC's manufacturing processes. The company spent a considerable amount of money preparing the land to meet Environmental Protection Agency (EPA) regulations for the disposal and storage of the toxic waste. Explain how this expenditure affects the hierarchy of the risk control measures being considered by the company's current management.

Educational Objective 7

Explain how climate change can increase risk for organizations.

Review Questions

7-1. Describe the litigation risks organizations may face in relation to climate change.

7-2. Describe six risk control measures an organization may take in relation to climate change.

7-3. Describe three types of insurance that risk managers should consider in relation to climate change.

7-4. Identify two risk transfer techniques that may be applied to climate change risk.

Application Question

7-5. Wind Sales, Inc. (WSI) has erected dozens of windmills on a hillside to generate electricity, which it sells to business and residential customers. WSI's risk manager is concerned that changing weather patterns will reduce the amount of wind needed to generate sufficient electricity. Describe a risk transfer method that might help treat this risk.

Educational Objective 8
Given information on an organization's environmental risk exposures, assess the risk and recommend treatment options.

Application Question

8-1. Midtown Recycling has purchased a vacant lot on which it plans to establish a recycling collection point. The treeless lot is unpaved, and a stream separates it from a residential area. Midtown plans to surface a driveway and drop-off area big enough for several vehicles to park briefly while unloading materials. Large, open bins will be provided for disposal of glass, aluminum, and plastic, and several large, covered dumpsters will be provided for paper and cardboard. A separate, open bin will be available for disposal of batteries. Midtown's business manager has been asked to complete an environmental risk assessment and treatment plan for the project.

   a.   Based on the information provided, identify at least one environmental risk exposure Midtown faces.

b. The business manager plans to retain experts to help assess the identified environmental risk exposures. Describe the information an expert could provide relative to the exposure(s) identified in a.

c. Recommend treatment options for the environmental loss exposure identified in a.

Answers to Assignment 9 Questions

NOTE: These answers are provided to give students a basic understanding of acceptable types of responses. They often are not the only valid answers and are not intended to provide an exhaustive response to the questions.

Educational Objective 1

1-1. These are examples of pollution liability:

   a. Example of negligence—Careless driving by the driver of an oil tank truck resulted in the truck's overturning and spilling its oil.

   b. Example of intentional tort—A factory discharged untreated chemicals into a stream, and property owners who lived downstream sued the factory owner for trespass.

   c. Example of strict liability—A toxic waste handler was held liable for injuries resulting from escape of hazardous waste even though the escape did not result from the handler's negligence.

1-2. Some environmental statutes contain provisions that make certain parties responsible for environmental injury even though they were not at fault or negligent.

1-3. An EPA evaluation considers these items:

   • The accountability of the board of directors for environmental matters

   • The assignment of environmental responsibility within senior management

   • The effective dispersion of responsibility through all levels of the organization

   • The day-to-day operation of the system in controlling activities that involve hazardous materials

1-4. These are the legal grounds that might be used to impose liability on the described polluters:

   a. Negligence. (The remodeler did not exercise the proper degree of care owed under the circumstances. Perhaps the remodeler should have used a lesser amount of cement or provided better ventilation of the area while he or she was working.)

   b. Nuisance. (The school district might allege that the emissions from the crematorium interfered with its students' right to enjoy public property.)

   c. The civic group might urge the city to take action against the polluter, alleging either nuisance or trespass (the physical deposition of the pollutants on the city's property).

Educational Objective 2

2-1. An organization might incur property losses as a result of environmental pollution because legal and financial consequences of pollution cleanup can reduce the net value of a property and make it difficult to sell. Spills and leaks may also result in inventory losses for an organization.

2-2. Personnel losses might arise as a result of environmental pollution because occupational exposure to hazardous materials can cause chemical burns or other on-the-job injuries. Also, many work environment contaminants have a cumulative effect on the body, resulting in illness or disease.

2-3. Net income losses might arise as a result of environmental pollution because any environmental contamination event is likely to result in some degree of business interruption, revenue reduction, negative press, and consumer boycotts. Under extreme circumstances, a shutdown may even be necessary. Significant expenses can also be incurred in environmental cleanup.

Educational Objective 3

3-1. These answers explain the purposes of certain environmental statutes:

a. The Clean Water Act seeks to improve the quality of surface waters by prohibiting or regulating the discharge of pollutants into navigable waters and restoring them to fishable and swimmable quality.

b. The Clean Air Act seeks to improve the quality of ambient air by regulating emissions from both mobile and stationary sources of air pollution. Parties that intend to construct or operate sources of air emissions are required to obtain permits to do so.

c. The purpose of the Motor Carrier Act of 1980 is to protect the environment from releases of harmful materials during transportation of such materials by motor carriers in interstate or intrastate commerce.

d. The Toxic Substance Control Act, enacted in 1976, regulates the chemical manufacturing industry and prevents the importation or manufacture of dangerous chemical substances without adequate safeguards to ensure that their use does not harm human health or the environment.

3-2. The purpose of the financial responsibility requirements under RCRA is to require permit holders to provide evidence that they have the financial resources to clean up any material from the facility that causes environmental damage and to compensate victims for bodily injury and property damage.

3-3. CERCLA's purpose is to facilitate the cleanup of abandoned or uncontrolled sites containing hazardous substances, including old dump sites.

3-4. OPA mandates that each party responsible for a vessel or facility from which oil is discharged (or is threatening to be discharged) into or upon navigable waters, adjoining shorelines, or the exclusive economic zone of the United States is liable for removal costs and damages.

Educational Objective 4

4-1. The three-step process can be summarized this way:

a. Identify what materials are present, the quantities of those materials, and the potentially harmful properties of the materials at the locations in question

b. Identify the potential routes those materials could take if they were released from or within the facility

c. Identify the target populations of living entities that could be affected if the identified materials followed the potential routes

4-2. These unique characteristics must be considered (answers may vary):

a. Environmental loss exposures tend to elude traditional exposure identification methods.

b. The amount of loss may be difficult to measure at a particular point in time.

c. Environmental losses are often very severe.

d. Many environmental remediation laws are funded in accordance with a "let the polluter pay" funding concept.

e. The amount of loss can increase substantially over time as the contamination migrates farther from its source.

4-3. Environmental loss exposures are often difficult to identify because they arise from activities that were conducted many years ago or may be created by extremely small quantities of substances that are difficult to detect or measure. Also, reviewing summaries of historical losses may not reveal any information on potential environmental claims. Similarly, physical inspections of facilities do not always reveal possible causes of environmental damage that may be buried or hidden from view.

4-4. As detection equipment is developed that can measure smaller quantities of contaminants, the loss exposure increases. In a cleanup project in which the goal is to achieve "nondetect" levels of a particular contaminant, a change in measuring technology could dramatically change the costs of the cleanup.

4-5. Internal and external resources include environmental compliance personnel within the organization, legal counsel, operational personnel who work with hazardous materials on a daily basis, environmental consultants, and employees of the federal or state Environmental Protection Agency (EPA).

Educational Objective 5

5-1. An organization might use environmental risk assessments in these ways:

- To improve the overall quality of its environmental risk control program

- To identify environmental liabilities assumed when property is transferred

- To determine the nature and extent of contamination

- To identify the best risk control measures to prevent further contamination

- To underwrite insurance

5-2. A quantitative environmental risk assessment identifies and analyzes numerical relationships between an exposure and the actual occurrence of adverse effects to human health or the environment (that is, it determines cause and effect). A qualitative risk assessment is used to identify and analyze either existing hazards, to remediate preexisting conditions, or potential hazards, to prevent environmental losses.

5-3. A risk management professional should consider these characteristics of a population at risk when evaluating existing or potential areas of contamination:

- Amount and extent of potential harm

- Number of the population affected

- Population concentration

- Vulnerability of each population to the exposure

- Value an organization or society places on the at-risk population

5-4. The environmental risk assessment process entails these four steps:

- Create an assessment plan

- Assemble the team

- Gather information to identify loss exposures

- Analyze environmental loss exposures

5-5. Amalgamated Paint Company's risk manager should have technical experts study the characteristics and behavior of the solvent in terms of the toxicity of potential wastes, releases, and discharges; the process inputs, such as raw materials and catalysts; and any byproducts produced. Pathways through which the solvent could travel if released, such as by ambient air, soils, surface water, and ground water, should be studied as well. Because of the proximity of residential development, the populations at risk should also be studied in terms of concentration and other characteristics. Finally, management practices should be studied. For example, what support can be anticipated or is needed from management for environmental loss control of this solvent?

Educational Objective 6

6-1. Source reduction includes these basic risk control measures:

- Changing or modifying equipment—improving the efficiency of production equipment to produce less pollution

- Substituting materials—replacing a hazardous material with a safer one or substituting materials to improve process efficiency and to produce less pollution

- Redesigning process—improving the fundamental way an operation is accomplished to produce less pollution

- Redesigning the product—changing the fundamental product characteristics and features of the manufacturing process to produce less pollution

- Changing operations or human behavior—changing established procedures and practices (for example, maintenance and housekeeping procedures) to produce less pollution

6-2. These answers describe how the given source treatment methods modify pollutants that have already been produced:

a. Recovery processes separate, remove, and concentrate reusable material from the waste.

b. Physical and chemical treatment processes reduce the volume of wastes, permit more economical and effective treatment, make waste less hazardous, and destroy toxic components of the waste.

c. Thermal processes dissolve wastes either through combustion or pyrolysis (chemical decomposition caused by heating in the absence of oxygen).

d. Biological processes use living organisms to treat waste.

6-3. These considerations can influence the selection of risk control measures to manage environmental loss exposures:

- The technical feasibility of the risk control measure

- The economic feasibility of the risk control measure

- The feasibility of the measure regarding environmental regulatory demands

6-4. Normally, disposal would be the last option recommended in the hierarchy of risk control measures, to be used only if all forms of source reduction and source treatment have been exhausted. However, because the cost of the disposal site has already been incurred in APC's case, current management may view disposal as the most economical option to use. Management may consider the option environmentally feasible because the company's disposal plans comply with EPA regulations. Nevertheless, management should consider the risk of introducing pollutants directly into the environment as well as the company's potential liability for any environmental harm that results from the toxic waste disposal.

Educational Objective 7

7-1. Organizations may face litigation for contributing to climate change. Such claims may arise from individual shareholder suits, class action suits, and regulatory agency actions. Stockholder lawsuits could focus on whether a company's officers and directors rendered a company unprofitable by failing to plan for climate change. Climate change mismanagement could become a more common type of litigation in class action lawsuits. Organizations may also face action by government agencies for failure to comply with environmental regulations.

7-2. Organizations may take these risk control measures in relation to climate change (any six):

- Appointment of team or individual to be responsible for climate change risk management—A person or team with a working knowledge of climate change should be appointed to address the climate change exposure.

- Risk avoidance—An organization may choose to withdraw from business areas that present climate change risk. An analysis of environmental costs and risks for various products or processes could reveal new market and product opportunities that may reduce climate change risk.

- Disclosure of financial risks—A detailed disclosure of an organization's climate change risks indicates a company's good-faith effort to measure, mitigate, and control climate change loss exposures. Such a disclosure may help encourage and retain investors.

- Disaster planning—Organizations must develop disaster planning for catastrophic events such as hurricanes, which may increase in frequency and intensity. These plans may include evacuation procedures, arrangements for alternative facilities, stockpiling of emergency supplies, and more frequent computer data backup.

- Reduction of greenhouse gases—Companies that emit greenhouse gases should assess their internal emissions reduction opportunities in comparison with externally available approaches.

- Energy conservation and alternate energy usage—Energy conservation can include actions such as installing energy-efficient windows, using energy-efficient lightbulbs, and adopting alternate energy approaches such as wind power and solar power.

- Adoption of "green" building measures and approaches—Structures can be built to promote energy conservation and use environmentally friendly construction products and processes such as geothermal heat pumps, rainwater collection, and radiant ceilings.

- Support for stricter building codes—Organizations should support and use stricter building codes that seek to prevent or reduce hurricane and other climate-related losses.

- Integration of climate change with overall business strategies—Climate change risk management decisions should be aligned with an organization's business strategies.

7-3. Risk managers should consider these types of insurance in relation to climate change:

- Commercial general liability—Whether climate change liability is covered under commercial general liability policies is uncertain; in some cases, coverage may depend on how the pollution exclusion is applied.

- Special environmental liability coverage—These policies may apply only when a causal connection is established between the insured's action and measurable harm.

- Directors and officers (D&O) liability insurance—Some D&O policies specifically exclude coverage for liability relating to climate change or global warming. Risk managers review D&O policy provisions that exclude or limit coverage for bodily injury or property damage, personal injury torts, or intentional misconduct to determine how such provisions might apply to climate change risk.

7-4. Two risk transfer techniques that may be applied to climate change risk are weather derivatives and carbon trading.

7-5. To mitigate WSI's losses resulting from insufficient wind to provide sufficient electrical power, WSI's risk manager might consider a weather derivative based on wind velocity. Such a derivative could be designed to pay an agreed-upon amount for each day within a designated period on which the average wind velocity fails to reach a designated average velocity.

Educational Objective 8

8-1. The following answers relate to Midtown Recycling's environmental risk assessment and treatment plan:

a. By providing a bin for disposal of batteries, Midtown faces an environmental risk that battery acid could be released into the soil and stream. If battery casings are damaged, acids and other chemicals could leak and be washed by heavy rains into the soil of the unpaved lot and, from there, to the stream. Heat from the sun could trigger a fire in the battery bin, which could spread to the paper recycling dumpsters, and winds could carry the smoke, including toxic fumes from some types of batteries, to the neighboring residential area.

b. An expert could provide information about the types of chemicals that could potentially be released from the batteries; their properties; their pathways as they are washed into the soil and the stream; and the degree and duration of danger they pose to populations at risk, such as neighboring residents. An expert could provide similar information about fumes from batteries released into the air by fire, including their types and properties, physical dangers of breathing them, their pathways based on wind patterns and direction, and degree of danger to populations at risk.

c. To prevent or reduce the risk of battery chemicals being washed into the soil and river, Midtown could surface the entire lot, use watertight containers with lids, and/or provide siphoned drainage to another container. To prevent or reduce the risk of release of chemical fumes into the air from fire, Midtown could use an inflammable, covered bin; place it away from direct sunlight; determine whether a fire-retardant substance could be added to the bin; position it far from containers of other flammable materials; and install a fire alarm or fire extinguishing system. Another risk treatment option is to eliminate batteries from the materials Midtown recycles.

Direct Your Learning

10

Crime and Cyber Risk

Educational Objectives

After learning the content of this assignment, you should be able to:

1. Describe the distinctive features of crime risk and their implications for risk management.

2. Describe the characteristics of common crimes.

3. Explain how to use risk control measures against crime losses.

4. Explain how an organization can have cyber risk loss exposures in each of the following categories:

   - Property

   - Net income

   - Liability

5. Explain how organizations can control or finance their cyber risk exposures.

6. Describe sources of social media risk and ways to control it.

Outline

▶ **Distinctive Features of Crime Risk**
  A. Hostile Intent
  B. Continual Evaluation of Risk Control Efforts
▶ **Characteristics of Common Crimes**
  A. Burglary
  B. Robbery
  C. Shoplifting
  D. Fraud
  E. Embezzlement
  F. Forgery and Counterfeiting
  G. Vandalism
  H. Arson
  I. Terrorism
  J. Espionage
  K. Computer Crime
▶ **Controlling Crime Losses**
  A. Crime Risk Control Measures
    1. Sound Personnel Policies
    2. Physical Controls
    3. Procedural Controls
    4. Managerial Controls
    5. Investigation and Prosecution of Crimes
  B. Reducing Scale of Crime and Recovery
▶ **Cyber Risk Loss Exposures**
  A. Property
    1. Loss of or Damage to Tangible Property
    2. Loss of or Damage to Intangible Property
  B. Net Income
    1. Loss of Business Income (Including Contingent Business Income)
    2. Extra Expense
  C. Liability
    1. Bodily Injury and Property Damage Liability
    2. Personal and Advertising Injury Liability
    3. Intellectual Property Liability
    4. Errors and Omissions Liability

▶ **Controlling and Financing Cyber Risk Loss Exposures**
  A. Risk Control Measures for Cyber Risk
    1. Physical Controls
    2. Procedural Controls
    3. Personnel Controls
    4. Managerial Controls
    5. Investigation and Prosecution of Cyber Crimes
    6. Post-Cyber Incident Rapid Recovery Program
  B. Risk Financing Measures for Cyber Risk
    1. Insurance
    2. Noninsurance Risk Transfer
    3. Retention
▶ **Social Media Risk**
  A. The Nature of Social Media
  B. Reputation Risk
  C. Legal Risk
    1. Employment Risks
    2. Security Risks
    3. Intellectual Property Risks
    4. Defamation
    5. Privacy Risks
  D. Operational Risk
  E. Controlling Social Media Risks

 If you are not sure that you have the current materials for the exam you plan to take, please contact The Institutes.

For each assignment, you should define or describe each of the Key Words and Phrases and answer each of the Review and Application Questions.

Educational Objective 1

Describe the distinctive features of crime risk and their implications for risk management.

Review Questions

1-1. Explain why risk control of crime losses differs from risk control of losses caused by accidents, negligence, or natural events.

1-2. Identify features of an organization that may present opportunities for crime.

1-3. Identify risk control measures that focus on taking precautions to eliminate weaknesses that make an organization a relatively easy crime target.

Application Question

1-4. Concerned about the accumulation of highly combustible paper trash, Sam, the building supervisor for a thirty-story office building, made sure the cleaning crew always hauled this trash away at the end of its late-night shift, 10 p.m. Between 9:30 and 10 p.m., however, a large accumulation of trash was usually visible. Explain how knowledge of the cleaning crew's procedures could affect the fire loss exposure of the building and its inhabitants.

Educational Objective 2
Describe the characteristics of common crimes.

Key Words and Phrases

Burglary

Robbery

Shoplifting

Fraud

Embezzlement

Forgery

Counterfeiting

Vandalism

Arson

Espionage

Computer crime

Computer sabotage

Review Questions

2-1. Distinguish between burglary, robbery, and shoplifting.

2-2. Describe the two broad types of crime losses caused by counterfeiters and forgers.

2-3. Describe the following types of computer crime exposures:

    a. Computer network breach

    b. Theft through hacking

    c. Theft of computer time

    d. Denial of service

Application Question

2-4. The risk manager at Greatview MegaStore has listed the organization's crime losses for the past quarter. Identify the crime associated with each of these losses.

    a. Greatview paid a $15,000 cash settlement to a customer who claimed to have slipped and fallen in the store's entryway. Later, film footage was discovered that showed the customer faking the fall.

    b. A disgruntled employee poured orange juice into five computers in Greatview's payroll office.

    c. Seventeen small kitchen appliances disappeared from the merchandise shelves.

    d. Unauthorized copies of Greatview gift cards were redeemed in exchange for $1,575 in merchandise.

e. Computer records documented that three office employees spent a total of seventy-five hours shopping online during work hours

f. Five flat screen televisions were stolen from the storage room; a door had been forced to gain entry.

Educational Objective 3
Explain how to use risk control measures against crime losses.

Key Word or Phrase

Perimeter system

Review Questions

3-1. Identify risk control measures that focus on deterrence and detection of crime.

3-2. Briefly describe how these physical controls can help reduce theft losses:

▶▶

a. Alarms

b. Security guards

c. Surveillance cameras

d. Locks, bars, and safes

3-3. Describe three managerial controls used to reduce criminal opportunity.

Application Question

3-4. Huntington Grocer has experienced a sharp increase in inventory shrinkage. The store manager suspects employee theft. Suggest personnel policies the store's risk management professional can implement to prevent or reduce the loss from this crime.

Educational Objective 4

Explain how an organization can have cyber risk loss exposures in each of the following categories:

- **Property**
- **Net income**
- **Liability**

Review Questions

4-1. Describe a cyber risk loss exposure.

4-2. Explain why, when cyber risk property loss exposures and standard coverage forms are considered, the distinction between tangible property and intangible property is important.

4-3. Explain how an organization with business income might be exposed to loss of contingent business income as a consequence of cyber risk.

4-4. Discuss how organizations may be exposed to cyber risk liability loss exposures.

4-5. Describe the categories of cyber risk liability loss exposures.

    a.   Discuss how cyber risk bodily injury liability loss exposures occur.

    b.   Discuss how cyber risk property damage liability loss exposures occur.

c. Discuss how cyber risk personal and advertising injury liability loss exposures occur.

d. Discuss how cyber risk intellectual property liability loss exposures occur.

e. Discuss how cyber risk errors and omissions liability loss exposures occur.

Application Question

4-6. Jim's Country Furniture and Crafts is a small, one-person business. Jim builds his own designs of country-styled furniture and crafts and sells them in his shop. Most of Jim's business is generated through referrals and repeat customers. Jim's wife performs the business's accounting tasks and other business-related record keeping. The business does not have a website. Jim believes that he does not have any cyber risk loss exposures. For each of the following scenarios, explain whether Jim has a cyber risk loss exposure:

a. Jim also designs architectural elements for homes, such as fireplace mantles, wall panels, and molding. To help in the design and assembly of large elements, Jim orders partially completed pieces from a supplier, who designs the pieces according to his specifications using computer aided design (CAD) technology.

b. Jim's wife relies on a home business software program that requires periodic Internet updates to manage Jim's accounts, billings, and other record keeping.

Educational Objective 5
Explain how organizations can control or finance their cyber risk exposures.

Key Words and Phrases

Biometrics

Denial-of-service attack

Hold-harmless agreement (or indemnity agreement)

Retention

Review Questions

5-1. Describe the benefits of a properly structured cyber risk security strategy.

5-2. Compare physical controls with procedural controls for cyber risk loss exposures.

5-3. Describe the personnel controls an organization can use to mitigate the cyber risk loss exposures presented by their employees.

5-4. Explain why organizations should continually evaluate and revise cyber risk control measures.

5-5. Discuss the reasons why an organization should report cyber crimes to authorities.

5-6. Identify the three methods of risk financing for cyber risk.

Application Question

5-7. Aaron, Becky, and Chuck have just formed an accounting partnership. They have a website to advertise the company and a computer system to prepare and maintain clients' financial records. When they meet with their insurance agent to set up their commercial package policy, including cyber risk insurance, they also discuss what they should do in the event of a cyber loss. Describe a post-cyber incident rapid recovery program for this company.

Educational Objective 6
Describe sources of social media risk and ways to control it.

Key Word or Phrase

Defamation

Review Questions

6-1. Identify ways an organization can benefit from use of social media.

6-2. Describe two ways an organization may be exposed to reputation risk through social media.

6-3. Explain why an organization's social media activities can increase its degree of exposure to legal risk.

6-4. Identify the circumstances under which an employer can legally base a hiring decision on personal information acquired from social media sources.

6-5. In addition to security breaches, describe a risk an organization faces from malicious software.

Application Question

6-6. The Human Resources (HR) Department at Northern Consolidated has developed a procedure for screening job applicants. For each applicant that survives initial screening, HR does a Web search of the applicant's name and also gathers personal information from that person's social media sites. The company has an opening for a position that requires long hours, extensive traveling, and heavy lifting. HR has rejected four candidates based on the information noted. Describe the employment risks, if any, Northern Consolidated faces because of these rejections.

   a. Candidate A writes a blog about raising his seven-year-old quadruplets.

   b. Candidate B posted a photo in which he is playing with his grandchildren.

c. A news article details Candidate C's arrest and conviction for selling prescription pain killers; tests indicated high levels of the medication in his blood.

d. Candidate D posted a photo of herself competing in gymnastics.

Answers to Assignment 10 Questions

NOTE: These answers are provided to give students a basic understanding of acceptable types of responses. They often are not the only valid answers and are not intended to provide an exhaustive response to the questions.

Educational Objective 1

1-1. Risk control measures for losses caused by accidents, negligence, or natural events may not be effective against crime losses. Effective risk control measures against crime losses must recognize that criminals are driven by hostile intent. Such measures should focus on eliminating opportunities for crime.

1-2. Features of an organization that may be particularly vulnerable to crime include these:

- High-value, easily transported items

- Unguarded property

- Vulnerable people

- Unprotected key operations

1-3. An organization can adopt these risk control measures that focus on taking precautions to eliminate weaknesses that make it a relatively easy crime target:

- Shield the organization's assets and activities by maintaining physical, procedural, and managerial barriers that reduce criminal opportunities

- Reduce criminals' perceptions that crimes can be committed without detection and punishment

1-4. An arsonist could use knowledge of the cleaning crew's procedures to light the trash accumulation on fire between 9:30 and 10 p.m. The presence of the cleaning crew in the building at that time presents an additional loss exposure because their lives would be endangered.

Educational Objective 2

2-1. In contrast to burglars, who normally steal property from buildings or unoccupied areas, robbers harm or threaten to harm people in order to steal from them. Neither shoplifters nor burglars use threat of force to steal directly from other people; however, shoplifters differ from burglars in that they are legitimately on the premises as customers, whereas burglars gain unauthorized access by breaking in.

2-2.   Counterfeiters and forgers can cause two broad types of crime losses:

- They can induce an organization to accept falsified currency, checks, credit cards, other negotiable instruments, documents, or artwork. When the organization exchanges something of value for the valueless items, the organization's immediate loss is the value of whatever it relinquished in the exchange.

- By creating or using unauthorized or stolen copies of the organization's own documents, they can impersonate the organization. Falsified documents can be used to manipulate funds, make seemingly valid promises, and issue "official" statements that harm the organization financially or damage its reputation.

2-3.   These are descriptions of computer crimes:

a.   Computer network breach—Vulnerable computer servers present loss exposures to computer operations because of their vital central administrative role within computer networks. Password protections to reduce such exposures can fail if passwords are revealed.

b.   Theft through hacking—Computer hackers typically steal data to learn trade secrets or to determine a competitor's marketing or financial strategy. Hackers may use computer viruses or "Trojan horses" that surreptitiously cull credit card data, passwords, or other sensitive information from an organization's systems.

c.   Theft of computer time—Unauthorized use by employees of computer time for personal purposes can occur when computer use is not supervised or audited.

d.   Denial of service—A denial-of-service attack prevents proper network communications. During such an attack, the organization's server may be flooded with so much incoming data that it crashes. The attackers may follow up with extortion e-mails. Alternatively, criminals may hack into customer databases and send out hundreds of thousands of e-mails illicitly, thereby wasting valuable computer time.

2-4.   These are the crimes associated with Greatview's crime losses:

a.   Settlement for customer's fall—fraud

b.   Orange juice on computers—computer sabotage

c.   Disappearance of small kitchen appliances—probably shoplifting

d.   Unauthorized copies of gift cards—counterfeiting

e.   Employee online shopping—theft of computer time

f.   Stolen televisions—burglary

Educational Objective 3

3-1. These risk control measures focus on deterrence and detection of crime:

- Sound personnel policies

- Physical controls

- Procedural controls

- Managerial controls

- Investigation and prosecution of crimes

3-2. Physical controls can help reduce theft losses in these ways:

a. Alarms detect intruders who have already entered the premises.

b. Security guards perform periodic patrols to ensure that the building structure and its contents are secure.

c. Surveillance cameras, by capturing crimes in progress on film, can facilitate the identification, conviction, and incarceration of criminals and can discourage crime.

d. Locks, bars, and safes restrict entry by delaying a thief's entrance.

3-3. Several kinds of managerial controls can be used to reduce criminal opportunity:

- Education informs employees about the organization's crime loss exposures, implemented risk control measures, and ways employees can help reduce crime losses.

- Applicant screening helps ensure that the organization hires and retains a reasonably suitable, trustworthy, and competent work force.

- Rotation of employees can deter crime by making employees aware that their crimes may be discovered after they are transferred.

3-4. The risk management professional should implement a personnel policy that requires background checks of potential employees, treats all employees fairly, resolves grievances promptly and equitably, and terminates or specifies other appropriate actions against employees who steal from the store. To implement these risk control measures, the risk management professional must work closely with human resources personnel because of the legal limitations imposed on organizations doing employee background checks.

Educational Objective 4

4-1. A cyber risk loss exposure is any condition that presents the possibility of financial loss to an organization from property, net income, or liability losses as a consequence of advanced technology transmissions, operations, maintenance, development, or support.

4-2. The distinction between tangible property and intangible property in relation to cyber risk property loss exposures is important because many commercial liability coverage forms define property damage to mean damage to tangible property and state that electronic data is not tangible property for coverage purposes. While commercial property forms do not typically make this distinction, they usually limit coverage for loss of electronic data. Consequently, a number of cyber risk loss exposures are not adequately covered, or not covered at all, by basic property and liability insurance policies.

4-3. An organization with business income might be exposed to loss of contingent business income as a consequence of cyber risk if it is dependent on income "contingent" on a location (such as key customers, suppliers, utilities, and third-party outsourcers) that it does not own or operate, and that location is exposed to cyber risk loss exposures. Typical loss exposures include computer network attack, virus, denial-of-service attack, sabotage, off-site power failure, failure of third party to properly manage and secure data, website defacement, and abuse of wireless networks.

4-4. Organizations that maintain a presence in cyber space may be exposed to cyber risk liability loss exposures. These exposures arise from using email, maintaining websites, developing software, and conducting business operations (such as sales and service) on the Internet.

4-5. The categories of cyber risk liability loss exposures are bodily injury and property damage liability, personal and advertising injury liability, intellectual property liability, and errors and omissions (E&O) liability.

   a. Cyber risk bodily injury liability loss exposures can occur because of an organization's software development. For example, a software developer develops a program for physicians and pharmacists regarding the potential adverse interactions of different prescription medications. Because of a formulary error in the program, physicians and pharmacists conclude that a particular combination of prescription drugs is safe when the combination actually produces a serious or fatal reaction in a number of patients. The patients and their families sue because of the bodily injury that resulted from the software error.

   b. Cyber risk property damage loss exposures can occur because of an organization's overall technology operations, including those related to software, hardware, electronic data, and other media. For example, an insurance industry software provider issues an updated version of its software to an insurance brokerage. However, because of a security failure that occurred when the software upgrade was developed and transmitted to the brokerage, upon installation the upgrade renders the brokerage's computer network inoperable, causing significant property damage to the system. The insurance brokerage then sues the software provider for the property damage to the network.

   c. Cyber risk personal and advertising injury liability loss exposures typically occur from an organization's websites, such as disparaging statements in online forums or false advertising.

   d. Cyber risk intellectual property liability loss exposures occur through the use of copyright or trademark infringement on an organization's website.

   e. Organizations that design and service computer networks and software have cyber risk errors and omissions liability loss exposures from errors or failures that result from their work. Other types of organizations that provide products or services over the Internet can also have cyber risk errors and omissions liability loss exposures related to the Internet transactions.

4-6. These answers describe Jim's cyber risk loss exposures.

   a.   Jim's business is exposed to a cyber risk loss exposure as a consequence of a key supplier's reliance on technology and software design. A failure in this technology could result in a failure of the supplier to forward needed materials to Jim, thus impairing his ability to design and build the architectural elements and consequently generate business income.

   b.   Cyber risk loss exposures may possibly exist as a consequence of the software program used by Jim's wife. Additionally, the business's reliance on the Internet for program updates can also present cyber risk loss exposures. If Internet access were impaired or prohibited because of power failure off site or a virus attack at the update source, for example, the update could not occur and the business would be operating with inaccurate information.

Educational Objective 5

5-1. Properly structured, a cyber risk security strategy can preserve an organization's resources, reduce the severity of losses that do occur, and hasten the organization's recovery from a cyber loss.

5-2. Physical controls place barriers between cyber criminals and their targets. Procedural controls specify that tasks be performed in secure ways that prevent or reduce losses.

5-3. Personnel controls include such measures as pre-employment screening, training, outlining unacceptable cyber behavior with associated consequences, and termination procedures that include revoking access and passwords.

5-4. As quickly as risk control measures are instituted to combat cyber risk, the technology that cyber criminals use to overcome them evolves. Therefore, organizations must be prepared to update their techniques accordingly.

5-5. An organization may experience a public relations benefit by voluntarily releasing the news regarding a cyber crime. Many law enforcement agencies possess expertise in cyber crime and help organizations control their loss exposures. Organizations that vigilantly investigate and prosecute cyber criminals are less likely to be viewed as easy targets by cyber criminals. Also, reporting certain types of cyber crimes may be required by state law.

5-6. Risk financing measures include insurance, noninsurance risk transfer, and retention.

5-7. A key risk control component for the accounting partnership's post-cyber incident rapid recovery program would include full backups of its computer system at an alternate location. Additionally, it should store all of its clients'—as well as the partnership's—financial and legal documents in fire-resistive containers. The company should plan contingency measures for computer equipment and access to client records in the event of a cyber incident. It should also have a plan to contact clients in the event of a cyber incident that affects client financial data.

Educational Objective 6

6-1. Organizations can use social media for these purposes (among others):

- To develop ongoing relationships with customers
- To create and convey a customer-friendly image that contributes to business success
- To disseminate information
- To provide customer service and feedback
- To monitor public perception of products and services and to respond quickly to significant changes in those perceptions—particularly negative ones
- To gather information about prospective employees
- To promote products or services
- To monitor social networks and blogs for reference to their own and their competitors' products and services

6-2. An organization may be exposed to reputation risk through social media in these ways:

- A single negative item of information—whether patently false, true, misinterpreted, or taken out of context—can reverse an organization's positive image and severely damage its reputation in a matter of hours, if not minutes.
- Employees may post negative comments about their employers, competitors, customers, or others associated with the organization or may inadvertently disclose confidential business information.

6-3. An organization's social media activities can increase its degree of exposure to legal risk because of the pervasiveness of social networking and the speed at which communication occurs.

6-4. In general, an employer can base a hiring decision on personal information acquired from social media sources if the information relates to behavior that would directly affect an applicant's job responsibilities.

6-5. Not only may an organization's security be breached by malicious software, but the organization could be held liable for failing to protect its clients' or customers' personal information.

6-6. Northern Consolidated faces these employment risks from rejecting applicants based on personal information acquired from the Internet:

a. The company could be accused of discriminating against Candidate A because of his family circumstances. With four young children, he might not want to travel or work long hours.

b. The company could be accused of discriminating against Candidate B on the basis of age.

c. The company may have legitimate reasons for rejecting Candidate C. His illegal use of pain killers while lifting heavy items could endanger himself and others, and the organization may have doubts about his reliability because of his behavior and criminal record.

d. The company could be accused of discriminating against Candidate D because of her gender and size; however, if it appears unlikely that she will be able to lift heavy objects, the company might be able to justify the rejection.

Direct Your Learning

Fleet Risk

Educational Objectives

After learning the content of this assignment, you should be able to:

1. Explain how fleets can be viewed as systems and the implications for fleet loss control.

2. Explain how Federal Motor Carrier Safety Regulations apply to motor vehicle fleets.

3. Explain how to control losses associated with the components of a motor vehicle fleet safety system.

4. Describe the technological advances in motor vehicle fleet safety.

Outline

▶ Fleets as Systems
   A. Components and Purpose
   B. Environment
   C. Life Cycle
   D. Systems and Relationships

▶ Federal Motor Carrier Safety Regulations
   A. Application to Fleet Operations
   B. Significant Rules
      1. Driver Qualification Rules
      2. Drug Testing for Employees Who Perform "Safety-Sensitive" Functions
      3. Hours of Service Rules
      4. Accident Reporting Rules
      5. Record Keeping Rules
      6. Electronic Device Usage Rules
   C. Compliance, Safety, and Accountability (CSA) Program

▶ Controlling Losses Associated With Motor Vehicle Safety Systems
   A. Vehicles
      1. Vehicle Selection
      2. Safety Equipment
      3. Vehicle Replacement
   B. Vehicle Maintenance
   C. Drivers
      1. Driver Selection
      2. Driver Training
      3. Driver Supervision
      4. Driver Licensing
      5. Driver Dismissal
   D. Cargoes
      1. Suitability to Vehicle
      2. Proper Loading
      3. Suitability of Routes
      4. Safeguards Against Inherent Vice
   E. Routes
   F. Vehicle Schedules

▶ Technological Advances in Motor Vehicle Fleet Safety
   A. Need for Technology
   B. Technological Advances

If you find your attention drifting, take a short break to regain your focus.

▶▶

For each assignment, you should define or describe each of the Key Words and Phrases and answer each of the Review and Application Questions.

Educational Objective 1
Explain how fleets can be viewed as systems and the implications for fleet loss control.

Review Questions

1-1. Describe characteristics an organization's fleet system should have to fulfill its purpose.

1-2. Describe how these environments might affect an organization's fleet safety:

a. Physical environment

b. Legal environment

  c. Economic environment

  d. Competitive environment

1-3. Identify two implications for risk control and fleet safety management regarding system relationships in an organization's fleet system.

Application Question

1-4. The management of Shirt Company, a shirt manufacturer, has decided the company will begin delivering its products to major retailers in the local area instead of contracting this service with a commercial delivery firm. Using the five-phase life cycle of a system, explain how Shirt Company's management and their risk management program can ensure appropriate delivery vehicles are selected and operate safely and efficiently.

Educational Objective 2

Explain how Federal Motor Carrier Safety Regulations apply to motor vehicle fleets.

Review Questions

2-1. List the reasons why a commercial motor vehicle (CMV) carrier/employer or driver may be required to undergo drug or alcohol testing.

2-2. Describe the three types of rest breaks that CMV drivers carrying property are required to take under the Federal Motor Carrier Safety Regulations (FMCSR) hours of service rules.

2-3. Explain how the Federal Motor Carrier Safety Administration (FMCSA) compliance, safety, and accountability (CSA) program uses Safety Measurement System (SMS) technology and describe the benefits recognized from the program.

Application Question

2-4. Ed works for a motor carrier and performs safety-sensitive duties. Following a ten-hour rest break, Ed reported to duty at 9:00 a.m. in his home terminal time zone. Ed spent his first two hours of on-duty time loading cylinders in his trailer. At 11:00 a.m., Ed's supervisor explained that his employer had randomly selected him for drug and alcohol testing and sent him to their designated testing facility. The testing and the travel time to and from the facility took an hour. Ed began his delivery at 12:00 p.m., and the drive is expected to take twelve hours.

   a. Explain how Ed's travel time for the drug and alcohol testing facility and the time for the testing are counted toward his on-duty time, according to the FMCSR.

   b. Based on his home-terminal time zone, at what time is Ed required to take a minimum thirty-minute rest break in accordance with the FMCSR hours of service rules? Explain your answer.

Educational Objective 3

Explain how to control losses associated with the components of a motor vehicle fleet safety system.

Review Questions

3-1. List the factors an organization should consider when selecting vehicles for its motor vehicle fleet.

3-2. Fleet driver supervision is difficult because drivers spend virtually all of their work time away from direct managerial observation. Identify some measures managers use to compensate for this lack of contact.

3-3. Describe motor vehicle safety considerations for controlling losses associated with cargo.

3-4. Identify the factors that help an organization plan routes that will control motor vehicle fleet losses.

Application Question

3-5. Shirt Company will begin making local deliveries within the next six months. Propose an operator selection process that will set the groundwork for safe and efficient operation of the delivery fleet.

Educational Objective 4

Describe the technological advances in motor vehicle fleet safety.

Review Questions

4-1. Describe two challenges organizations face that support the need for technology to safeguard motor vehicles and their cargo.

4-2. Explain the consequence of an organization not acting on data captured by an onboard computer that indicates a driver frequently acts in an unsafe manner.

4-3. Explain how real-time tire pressure monitors and onboard tire inflation systems improve commercial motor vehicle fleet safety in general, and particularly to eight-wheeled vehicles with "run flat" tires.

Application Question

4-4. Shirt Company has expanded its distribution area to include areas throughout the United States. Vehicle operators are on the road for longer shifts and operate with little direct supervision regarding safe driving practices. Explain how management, in their risk control efforts, might use advanced technology to monitor and improve fleet safety.

Answers to Assignment 11 Questions

NOTE: These answers are provided to give students a basic understanding of acceptable types of responses. They often are not the only valid answers and are not intended to provide an exhaustive response to the questions.

Educational Objective 1

1-1. To fulfill its purpose, an organization's fleet system should have these characteristics:

- Reliable—The fleet completes trips as scheduled without harm to the freight or passengers.

- Safe and well maintained—The fleet incurs few, if any, vehicle accident losses that might increase transport time because of vehicle repair or maintenance.

- Efficient—The fleet operates at an acceptable cost.

- Environmentally neutral—The fleet's operation does not pollute or harm the environment in ways that can impose common law or statutory liability.

- Lawful—The fleet operates within the legal requirements of local, state, and federal laws.

1-2. These answers address how the described environments might affect an organization's fleet safety:

a. Highways, weather conditions, terrain, communities, and other forces encountered along a route can affect safe operation.

b. Laws, such as those regarding speeds, weights, hours of service, mandated equipment, and operator licensing, tend to raise the level of fleet safety. Fleet managers may need to spend time ensuring operation within the law.

c. During prosperity, fleet safety is likely to be financially supported by adequate budgets. In recessionary periods, budgets may be cut, encouraging operators to speed, drive extra hours, or skip safety checks; vehicle maintenance may become haphazard to cut costs. In addition, labor union strikes and civil disorders might threaten safe delivery of cargoes.

d. Intense competition might lower fleet safety efforts and expenditures. These cost control measures could jeopardize the long-term safety of vehicles, operators, and their cargoes.

1-3. These are two implications for risk control and fleet safety management regarding system relationships:

- When a smaller system fails, it becomes more likely that each of the larger systems of which the smaller system is part will also fail. Because many of those failures cause accidents, they are a central risk control concern.

- The failure of the larger system degrades the environment in which its subsystems operate, increasing the strain on those subsystems and the probability that they will fail. Accidents become more likely.

1-4. Shirt Company might apply the five-phase life cycle in this way:

- Conceptual phase—evaluate the types of delivery vehicles required, along with possible routes and schedules

- Engineering phase—select reliable delivery vehicles, select and train operators, finalize routes and delivery schedules, plan appropriate vehicle maintenance, and educate operators and others on accident procedures

- Production phase—purchase the delivery fleet vehicles

- Operational phase—implement and monitor measures that control the overall cost of risk (insurance costs, safety measures, and administrative costs) attributable to the organization's fleet operations

- Disposal phase—eliminate old vehicles unable to legally fulfill the purposes and attributes of the fleet because of age, technological obsolescence, or other reasons and replace those vehicles with vehicles that better fulfill the organization's transportation needs; retire or reassign employees no longer qualified to operate their vehicles

Educational Objective 2

2-1. A CMV carrier/employer or driver may be required to undergo drug or alcohol testing for any of these reasons:

- Pre-employment

- Random

- Reasonable suspicion/reasonable cause

- Post-accident

- Return-to-duty

- Follow-up

2-2. Under the FMCSR hours of service rules, CMV drivers that carry property are required to take a minimum ten-hour, off-duty break after the fourteenth consecutive hour of on-duty time. They are required to take a minimum thirty-minute rest break after every eight hours of on-duty time. And they are additionally required to take a minimum thirty-four-hour, off-duty break, including specified early morning hours, after they reach their weekly maximum on-duty hours, which vary depending on whether the carrier operates six or seven days per week.

2-3. The FMCSA's CSA program uses SMS technology to track and update safety performance data collected through roadside inspections, safety-based violations, state-reported accidents, and the federal motor carrier census to quantify carriers' performance and assign a safety score. Tools are used to evaluate the reasons for safety problems. Officials use this information to recommend remedies, to encourage corrective action, and, if inadequate, to access penalties. The CSA has led to more efficient and effective intervention and the ability to reach more carriers than was possible with compliance reviews; carriers are also better able to identify and correct their own safety issues.

2-4. These answers are based on Ed's case:

    a. Under the FMCSR, on-duty time includes time associated with providing a carrier's required alcohol or drug testing, including travel time. Consequently, Ed would include that hour as on-duty time when determining his hours of service to meet FMCSR requirements.

    b. In accordance with the FMCSR hours of service rules, Ed is required to take a minimum thirty-minute rest break at 5:00 p.m. in his home terminal time zone. Ed's on-duty time includes the time he loaded his trailer and the time he participated in the required drug and alcohol testing, along with his driving time.

Educational Objective 3

3-1. These are factors an organization should consider when selecting vehicles for its motor vehicle fleet:

- Intended use of the vehicle

- Safety record of the vehicles

- Ease of maintenance

- Uniformity among vehicles

3-2. Managers of larger common carriers often compensate for lack of contact with their drivers through procedural and physical controls, such as requiring that drivers keep a written log of times when they leave or arrive at particular stops, or require a precise route and driver phone calls at predetermined times to report their locations. Two-way radios or cell phones allow random contact and monitoring. Automatic devices in some fleets make continuous-time recordings of vehicle speed and direction and times when the vehicle is stopped; some are submitted through real-time, electronic reporting. Managers of smaller fleets use less-formal methods, such as holding meetings or riding along. Some fleet managers offer rewards for outstanding performance or discipline for substandard performance.

3-3. These motor vehicle safety considerations control losses associated with cargo:

- Suitability to vehicle—Some cargoes require special vehicles because of the cargo's characteristics, weight, corrosiveness, or toxicity.

- Proper loading—Overloading or failure to properly secure cargo might result in cargo damage, vehicle damage, missed delivery schedules, or accidents.

- Suitability of routes—Routes should present no unreasonable risk to the cargo, and the cargo should present no unreasonable risk to properties or persons along the route.

- Safeguards against inherent vice—The vehicle must provide the appropriate environment for the cargo, and specially designed environmental controls must be working in a manner that nothing will jeopardize that environment.

3-4. Routes that help control motor vehicle fleet losses include those that are safe, cost-effective, reliable, and reasonable in distance and that offer some flexibility if the main route is blocked or closed.

3-5. Shirt Company should first analyze the job functions to establish specific operator qualifications. In the recruitment process, company risk control managers might encourage the use of applications listing licenses, work history, and driving records, which can provide a method of pre-screening to eliminate unsuitable or high-risk applicants. In the process of interviewing, the company's risk management professional might require administration of physical, written, and driving tests. Reference checks and verification of driving credentials should occur before the job offer is completed. Once hired, the organization should provide orientation and training for the employee, and it should maintain qualification files on each employee/driver.

Educational Objective 4

4-1. Two challenges organizations face that support the need for technology to safeguard motor vehicles and their cargo are driver error, the most frequent cause of motor vehicle accidents, and minimal driver supervision because of driver mobility, which makes knowing whether drivers are engaging in risky behaviors or whether they are exceeding the federal hours of service requirements for commercial motor vehicles difficult for management.

4-2. The consequence of not acting on data captured by an onboard computer could be liability imposed on the organization, especially if the driver's unsafe behavior leads to the driver being involved in an accident.

4-3. Real-time tire pressure monitors alert commercial motor vehicle drivers to improperly inflated tire conditions that can cause excessive tire wear, loss of fuel efficiency, and unsafe driving conditions. Particularly, eight-wheeled vehicles with "run flat" tires use these monitors to alert drivers to a flat tire and the need to decrease speed and seek an appropriate repair location. Onboard tire inflation systems keep proper air pressure in select tires to reduce the chance that drivers will lose control of their vehicles.

4-4. To establish safety monitoring methods, Shirt Company's management might install onboard computers that provide feedback regarding reckless vehicle operation, equipment malfunctions, and violations of Federal Motor Carrier Safety Regulation (FMCSR) hours-of-service rules. Stability control systems, rear- and dash-mounted video cameras, antilock braking systems, collision warning systems, tire pressure and inflation systems, onboard scales, and global positioning systems might be installed to provide more detailed safety information to the driver, improve the safe operation of the fleet, reduce or eliminate certain types of accidents, and help Shirt Company avoid payment of fraudulent claims.

Exam Information

About Institutes Exams

Exam questions are based on the Educational Objectives stated in the course guide and textbook. The exam is designed to measure whether you have met those Educational Objectives. The exam does not necessarily test every Educational Objective. It tests over a balanced sample of Educational Objectives.

How to Prepare for Institutes Exams

What can you do to prepare for an Institutes exam? Students who pass Institutes exams do the following:

▶ Use the assigned study materials. Focus your study on the Educational Objectives presented at the beginning of each course guide assignment. Thoroughly read the textbook and any other assigned materials, and then complete the course guide exercises. Choose a study method that best suits your needs; for example, participate in a traditional class, online class, or informal study group; or study on your own. Use The Institutes' SMART Study Aids (if available) for practice and review. If this course has an associated SMART Online Practice Exams product, you will find an access code on the inside back cover of this course guide. This access code allows you to print a full practice exam and to take additional online practice exams that will simulate an actual credentialing exam.

▶ Become familiar with the types of test questions asked on the exam. The practice exam in this course guide or in the SMART Online Practice Exams product will help you understand the different types of questions you will encounter on the exam.

▶ Maximize your test-taking time. Successful students use the sample exam in the course guide or in the SMART Online Practice Exams product to practice pacing themselves. Learning how to manage your time during the exam ensures that you will complete all of the test questions in the time allotted.

Types of Exam Questions

The exam for this course consists of objective questions of several types.

The Correct-Answer Type

In this type of question, the question stem is followed by four responses, one of which is absolutely correct. Select the *correct* answer.

Which one of the following persons evaluates requests for insurance to determine which applicants are accepted and which are rejected?

a.   The premium auditor

b.   The loss control representative

c.   The underwriter

d.   The risk manager

The Best-Answer Type

In this type of question, the question stem is followed by four responses, only one of which is best, given the statement made or facts provided in the stem. Select the *best* answer.

Several people within an insurer might be involved in determining whether an applicant for insurance is accepted. Which one of the following positions is primarily responsible for determining whether an applicant for insurance is accepted?

a.   The loss control representative

b.   The customer service representative

c.   The underwriter

d.   The premium auditor

The Incomplete-Statement or Sentence-Completion Type

In this type of question, the last part of the question stem consists of a portion of a statement rather than a direct question. Select the phrase that *correctly* or *best* completes the sentence.

Residual market plans designed for individuals who are unable to obtain insurance on their personal property in the voluntary market are called

a.   VIN plans.

b.   Self-insured retention plans.

c.   Premium discount plans.

d.   FAIR plans.

"All of the Above" Type

In this type of question, only one of the first three answers could be correct, or all three might be correct, in which case the best answer would be "All of the above." Read all the answers and select the *best* answer.

When a large commercial insured's policy is up for renewal, who is likely to provide input to the renewal decision process?

a.   The underwriter

b.   The loss control representative

c.   The producer

d.   All of the above

"All of the following, EXCEPT:" Type

In this type of question, responses include three correct answers and one answer that is incorrect or is clearly the least correct. Select the *incorrect* or *least correct* answer.

All of the following adjust insurance claims, EXCEPT:

a.   Insurer claims representatives

b.   Premium auditors

c.   Producers

d.   Independent adjusters